We Have Fed You All For A Thousand Years

words: An Unknown Proletarian
music: Mat Callahan

1.

We have fed you all for a thousand years
And here we are still unfed
But there's never a dollar of all your wealth
That's doesn't mark the workers dead
We have given our best to give you rest
And you lie on crimson wool
But if blood be the price of all your wealth
Then good God we have paid in full

2.

There is never a mine blown skyward now
But we're buried alive for you
There is never a wreck drifts shoreward now
But we are its ghastly crew
Go reckon our dead by the forges red
And the factories where we spin
Lord, if blood be the price of your cursed wealth
Good God we have paid it in

3.

We have fed you all for a thousand years
For that was our doom, you know
From the days when you chained us in your fields
To the strike a week ago
You have taken our lives, and our babies and wives
And we're told it's your legal share
But if blood be the price of your lawful wealth
Then good God we have bought it fair

Come On Friends And Let's Go Down

words: Sarah Ogan Gunning
music: "The Good Ol' Way" (unknown author)

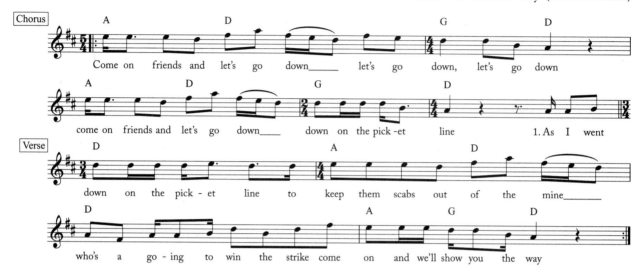

1.

As I went down on the picket line
To keep them scabs out of the mine
Who's a going to win the strike
Come on and we'll show you the way

CHORUS

2.

Went out one morning before daylight
And I was sure we'd have a fight
But the capitalist scurvy'd run away
And we went back the very next day

CHORUS

3.

We all went out on the railroad track
To meet them scabs and turn them back
We win that strike I'm glad to say
Come on, and we'll show you the way

CHORUS

ACKNOWLEDGMENTS

We especially want to thank the following people for their invaluable assistance:

Jay Blakesberg for assistance in gaining access to Jim Marshall's lovely photo of Sarah Ogan Gunning and Pete Seeger

Tinya Seeger for providing photos of Sarah Ogan Gunning, Jim Garland, and John Handcox from her father's personal collection

Eli Smith for his help in conceiving this project and launching it at the Brooklyn Folk Festival

Steve Garabedian and Franz Morrissey for their insightful reading and thoughtful criticism in the preparation of this book

WORKING-CLASS
HEROES

WORKING-CLASS HEROES

A History of Struggle in Song
A Songbook

Edited by **Mat Callahan and Yvonne Moore**

2019

Working-Class Heroes: A History of Struggle in Song: A Songbook
© Mat Callahan and Yvonne Moore
This edition © 2019 PM Press

ISBN: 978-1-62963-702-0
Library of Congress Control Number: 2019933002

Cover by John Yates/stealworks.com
Layout by Jonathan Rowland

Photo Credits
Mat and Yvonne photo: Karl-Heinz Hug, www.hugphotos.com
Sarah Ogan Gunning and Pete Seeger Photo: © Jim Marshall Photography LLC
John Handcox photo: Pete Seeger personal collection; photographer unknown
Jim Garland photo: Pete Seeger personal collection; photographer unknown
Paul Robeson illustration: Charles Henry Alston, 1907-1977, Artist (NARA record: 3569253), https://en.wikipedia.org/
wiki/Charles_Alston

PM Press
PO Box 23912
Oakland, CA 94623
www.pmpress.org

10 9 8 7 6 5 4 3 2 1

CONTENTS

Introduction

It was the end of the year 2016 when I had a conversation with an old friend, Eli Smith. Eli is a fine musician and devoted archivist of old-time string band music. He also happens to be the organizer of the Brooklyn Folk Festival where Yvonne and I performed James Connolly's *Songs of Freedom* in 2016. At first, Eli and I were just "shooting the breeze" about family and friends when we hit upon the subject of commemorations. I happened to mention that 2017 would be the fiftieth anniversary of the publication of *Hard Hitting Songs for Hard-Hit People*, a songbook first published in 1967 after a thirty-year odyssey through the desk drawers and cupboards of two of its authors, Woody Guthrie and Pete Seeger. I knew the songbook well, having obtained a copy when it first came out. Eli wasn't born yet, but he too knew all about this book and its striking relevance to present-day social and musical developments. We immediately agreed that it would be a worthwhile task to select, from among the book's 195 songs, a representative sample for performance at the 2017 Brooklyn Folk Festival.

Yvonne and I had to choose an hour's worth of tunes that we thought would connect with an audience unfamiliar with the book or the historical period on which it was based, that is, 1910–1940, with the bulk of the songs being written in the '30s. The music and the lyrics had to cross the divide of almost a century to speak again to a new generation. So we set to work with more curiosity than conscious plan.

As soon as we began, however, certain patterns emerged. First, these songs were composed by workers, not professional musicians or lyricists. While some were written by Woody Guthrie, the great majority were by anonymous working people who shared one thing in common: the struggle against suffering and injustice. The songs of Sarah Ogan Gunning are a shining example. They are stunning lyrically and had the curious advantage of being set to music recently popularized by the Coen Brothers film *O Brother, Where Art Thou?*. Second, the songs of Sarah's brother and sister, Jim Garland and Aunt Molly Jackson, were equally powerful, calling attention to the

Kentucky coal country where all three were born and participated in great struggles against the coal operators. These facts alone exposed the falsehoods that have been foisted on unwitting music lovers for decades, namely that the working class was a bunch of dumb crackers, that "political" songs were all written by intellectuals in New York, and that "real" working-class songs were either maudlin laments about life's misfortunes or carefree larks admonishing listeners to "keep on the sunny side of life." Needless to say, this is hokum, but more importantly, the evidence proving that it is hokum is truly wonderful music, and fun, to boot.

Shortly thereafter, our song-quest brought us to more such people, Ella May Wiggins and John Handcox, to name but two, who were not only workers and organizers themselves but were songwriters of merit, putting their talents to the task of building the workers' movement. To these we added a few written by the better-known, but equally "authentic," Joe Hill and Ralph Chaplin. These songs were found in *Hard*

Ella May's children orphaned after her murder (LEFT TO RIGHT) Albert, 3; Myrtle, 11; Chalady, 13 months; Clyde, 8; and Millie, 6.

Hitting Songs for Hard-Hit People even though they were from an earlier era and had already been disseminated widely by the Wobblies (Industrial Workers of the World). Then, with our repertoire complete, we played the Brooklyn Folk Festival.

That might have been the end of it, but serendipitously we were asked to perform at several other festivals, notably the James Connolly Festival in Dublin, later in 2017. What followed were more concerts, longer than a festival set, which required that we return to the songbook for more material. Ultimately, we had two hours' worth of songs and rich stories accompanying each one. These stories included not only the struggles that had inspired the songs but also those of the people who'd written them. After many performances in the U.S., Ireland, Germany, and Switzerland, it became apparent that diverse audiences shared an intense interest in both the music and the stories. The beauty and emotional power of the songs was immediate and produced the effect of transporting people to the time and place of their origin. But something else touched them as well. Not only were many audience members deeply moved by the music but they were also curious to know more about the people who created it. Aficionados of "Americana" were especially intrigued. How could it be that they didn't know about these songs? Why were they not included in the compilations and collections claiming to be "representative" or "definitive"? And their authors? Who were they, and why are they not remembered?

It was early this year, 2018, that we realized the necessity of recording the music, transcribing it for others to sing and sharing, in printed form, the stories we'd been telling from the stage. Since by this time we were no longer strictly confined to songs from *Hard Hitting Songs for Hard-Hit People, and* because that book is still readily available (and should be enjoyed in its own right), we decided to focus on what to us was the most important aspect of the project, namely the people who made these songs and the cause they made them for. These are women and men who gave their lives to emancipate the working class. Many, like Ella May Wiggins, were literally murdered by the bosses. Others, like Sarah Ogan Gunning, watched their children starve to death and their husbands die of black lung, only to rise up singing against the system that caused so much misery. This is why we call our project *Working-Class Heroes*.

Unlike mythical figures made in Hollywood or celebrities made by marketing, these were real human beings, ordinary, anonymous, and poor. Their heroism resulted not from their being different than their fellow workers, but from being the same. The same, that is, except in one respect: lowly of birth, they were nonetheless noble of aspiration. They stood up, calling out to their sisters and brothers to join together to fight the bosses, the bankers, and the government that were oppressing them. They did so in the face of violent terror and bitter betrayal, their dedication and courage setting an example we can learn from today. Such heroism is immortal, such heroes should be celebrated, and their songs can still lift our spirits, if we sing them.

THERE IS MEAN THINGS HAPPENING IN THIS LAND

THE SONGS WE CHOSE HAVE SPECIFIC CHARACTERISTICS THAT MAKE THEM PARTIC-ularly timely today, as is illustrated by John Handcox's "There Is Mean Things Happening In This Land." But this goes beyond their lyrics or melodies to the facts of their origin and the purposes to which they were originally put. These origins and purposes make these songs more than mere relics of a bygone era or curiosities of an "old, weird America." As songs and as evidence, they challenge many widely accepted notions concerning music, history, and politics.

For example, it might at first appear that these songs are anomalies or that *Hard Hitting Songs* is merely the product of Lomax's, Guthrie's, and Seeger's ideologi-cal bias. In fact, there is an inexhaustible supply of such songs. We chose these not because they were exceptional or rare but because they are exemplary and typical. A similar collection could have been made from songs written by Filipino, Chinese, Japanese, and Mexican agricultural workers on strike in California at the same time the Harlan County War was raging. A collection could have been drawn from songs composed by autoworkers in Michigan and Ohio, sharecroppers in Alabama, or maritime workers on the Atlantic and Pacific Coasts. At the very moment Aunt Molly Jackson and John Handcox were composing their lyrics, the United States was convulsed with a workers' uprising of unprecedented size and scope. And this was in conjunction with struggles raging in many parts of the world. Indeed, it's the national and international impact of these struggles, more than any local dimension, that gave them their greatest significance. Why should it surprise us that songs would be written by the people involved?

We stuck to the time period and geographical parameters set by *Hard Hitting Songs* not due to any romantic attachment to coal mining, the South, or the 1930s, but because there are striking similarities between the first three decades of the twentieth century and the first two of the twenty-first. Deep systemic crisis, advancing fascism, the threat of world war—these are ominous symptoms making comparison inevitable.

5

So, too, are efforts to divide the working class—even to deny it exists—especially along the ages-old black/white divide, but also along the divide of Americanism vs. everyone else that typified the early part of the twentieth century.

But if these songs are timely now, they were above all timely when they were created. By and large, they were composed in the heat of battle and were meant to serve immediate needs, not to become "classics" of a "genre," let alone monuments to their composers. Nevertheless, their relevance to current affairs invites us to explore the historical conditions that inspired their creation. We found not only that the "mists of time" enshroud the period but that a host of misconceptions and falsehoods have obscured them as well.

Clearing the Fog

Fortunately recent scholarship has begun to penetrate the fog. Several books published since the late '90s provide not only important data but analysis that puts persistent controversies in a new light. Two outstanding examples are *The Cultural Front: The Laboring of American Culture in the Twentieth Century*, by Michael Denning, and *American Folk Music and Left-Wing Politics, 1927–1957*, by Richard and JoAnne Reuss. Both books first of all acknowledge that the Russian Revolution, the Communist Party and efforts to organize the workers of the United States are factors contributing to music and other artistic expressions that are now commonly referred to as American. Second, both take into account the role of anticommunism as more than simply a predictable response to the Red Menace on the part of capitalists, exposing it as an ideological formation independent of anything the CPUSA or the USSR may have said or done. Indeed, anticommunism has little to do with communism as a philosophical or political idea, instead using the word as a synonym for unspeakable evil or infectious disease. Propagated by A. Mitchell Palmer in the First Red Scare of 1919, anticommunism became the founding principle for J. Edgar Hoover and the FBI, America's secret police. The purpose of anticommunism was, above all, to crush working-class resistance, but it had the further task of making it appear that such resistance never occurred and that even the existence of classes is a figment of deluded imaginations. This strategy brings to mind John Lennon's "Working Class Hero," where he sings, "Keep you doped with religion and sex and TV/And you think you're so clever and classless and free." This furthermore helps explain many of the misconceptions that have developed subsequently regarding the period and the music that emerged from it.

Perhaps the biggest misconceptions surround the Great Depression. There is no question that the Crash of '29 and the misery that followed were of epic proportions. It's no wonder so many pundits compared the financial crisis of 2008 to its predecessor. But this is far from the whole story. The period would more accurately be characterized by massive protests such as the Bonus Army March or the Farmer's Holiday Movement but most significantly by wave upon wave of strikes.[1] "If 1929 became a symbol of despair and ruin, an emblem of the crash of an economy and a way of life," writes Michael Denning, "1934 stands as one of the lyric years in American history . . . an emblem of insurgency, upheaval, and hope." In 1934, San Francisco, Minneapolis, and Toledo were rocked by general strikes. Longshore and maritime workers in the first, teamsters in the second, and auto parts workers in third led militant resistance to employers' attacks, shutting down entire cities and demonstrating the power of organized labor. Also in 1934, four hundred thousand textile workers from Maine to Alabama, walked out while in California agricultural workers staged the largest agricultural strikes in American history. Not all these battles ended in victory for the workers. But they nonetheless were part of a social movement that was to profoundly affect public policy and popular culture for decades to come. This provides a basis for understanding the optimism and fighting spirit of the songs in this collection. It is also convincing evidence of the enthusiasm with which workers at the time must have received them.

Another misconception concerns the role of communism in general, and the CPUSA in particular. Within living memory, this subject inspired heated debate in the realms of politics and music. As recently as the 1960s, the subject of folk music and figures such as Pete Seeger, Woody Guthrie, and Paul Robeson were all embroiled in this controversy, which of course related to the fact that the Soviet Union still existed. Now Robeson's and Guthrie's visages grace U.S. postage stamps. Seeger performed at the inauguration of Barack Obama. It would appear that with the collapse of communism in 1991, the system has indeed "moved on" and can now

---

[1] The Bonus Army March was launched by veterans of World War I to demand the bonuses they were promised for their service. In 1932 at least fifty thousand people converged on Washington, DC, setting up a tent city and causing great consternation among ruling elites. It was violently dispersed by U.S. troops led by General Douglas MacArthur.

The Farmer's Holiday Association was a movement calling on farmers to withhold produce from the market. A popular song summarized its views: "Let's call a Farmer's Holiday, a Holiday let's hold. We'll eat our wheat and ham and eggs, and let them eat their gold."

WEATHER
Rain
And
Cooler

Daily Worker

★
Star
Edition

Reentered as second class matter Oct. 22, 1947, at the post office at New York, N. Y., under the Act of March 3, 1879

Vol. XXVI, No. 171   New York, Monday, August 29, 1948   (12 Pages) Price 5 cents

LYNCH MOB RUNS AMUCK AT ROBESON CONCERT

PAUL ROBESON

By Joseph North

PEEKSKILL, N. Y., Aug. 28.—A mob of 300 vandals inflamed by the newspapers and official hysteria ambushed an out-door concert where Paul Robeson was to sing Saturday night, burned a Klan cross, and assaulted hundreds of men, women and children. They shouted "Hitler was okay, only he didn't finish the job." Brandishing clubs and hurling rocks, the

mobsters were abetted by Albany and local authorities who knew danger was brewing throughout the week but who refused to adopt a single measure of prevention. On the contrary, some helped to prepare the night's terror. I heard hoodlums shout on the state highway fronting the picnic grounds, "Where's Robeson, let's get Robeson. We'll kill the n——."

Scenes you saw of brownshirts burning books at Nuremberg were reenacted here in the quiet Hudson Valley a few scant miles from the home where Franklin D. Roosevelt lived.

Police, local and state, conveniently absented themselves until most of the damage was done. Some local sheriffs were seen to mingle with the mob while it ran amuck.

DEWEY KNEW

Governor Dewey knew about it: his State Attorney General Nathaniel Goldstein knew trouble was in the air days in advance. Local progressives had wired him as long ago as last Wednesday. Herbert Gerlach, leading official of Westchester County, knew about it the same time. He informed the local progressives and the committee that sponsored the affair on behalf of the Harlem Chapter of the Civil Rights Congress that all necessary police protection would be on hand. A cultural organization, People's Artists, sponsored the concert.

Instead, mothers had babies snatched from their arms; some women were shoved into a nearby swimming pool; others were manhandled, their clothes torn from them. Men were bludgeoned by gangs that outnumbered them 10 to one. Fourteen automobiles were overturned, many while their occupants were still inside.

CROSS BURNED

A burning cross flared into the night at 8:15 a few yards from the stage. Raging like madmen, the hoodlums made a bonfire of the chairs and fed it with sheets of the music that was to be sung.

It was Hitler Germany all over again. The harm would have been even greater had it not been for the heroic stand of the men and women inside the picnic grounds who had come early.

Four times a courageous group of 42 men, Negro and white, locked arms and resisted the entry of the howling gang that numbered between 300 to 400.

The men inside were protecting the women and children who stood near the platform, about a quarter mile inside the grounds. Howard Fast, the writer, was among the men who held back the gangs. Scheduled to act as master of ceremonies, Fast played a big part in helping to prevent the hoodlums from further harming the women and children.

Most of those trapped inside the picnic grounds were young men and women who had come to help arrange the affair. They included local progressives and others who came from New York City by bus.

MANY INJURED

Many of them today are suffering serious injuries, struck by rocks, fists and clubs. But they held back the hoodlums for several hours until the cars of several thousand who came to attend the concert lined up outside the grounds. And until the state police finally—at 10 o'clock—came.

The hoodlums carefully planned their strategy. They began arriving about 7 p.m. The concert was scheduled to begin at 8.

They built a three-foot barricade of large stones about the single entry and exit to the grounds. Jeering, threatening, they prevented cars from entering the grounds, (Continued on Page 9)

Investigate Mob, Jackie Says

By Bill Mardo

Jackie Robinson, from his bench in the Brooklyn Dodger dugout yesterday afternoon bitterly blasted the fascist-inspired mob riot at Peekskill.

ROBINSON

"Paul Robeson should have the right to sing, speak or do anything he wants to," said the Dodgers' Negro ace, who hadn't heard of the Peekskill riot until handed a newspaper report by this writer.

After reading slowly and carefully every word of the story, Robinson put the paper down and said angrily, "Those mobs make it tough on everyone.

"Its Robeson's right to do or be or say as he believes. They say here in America you're allowed to be whatever you want.

"I think those rioters ought to be investigated and let's find out if what they did is supposed to be the democratic way of doing things."

The newspaper version, was heavily larded with the usual red-baiting.

Observing that Communism wasn't the issue in what happened at Peekskill, Robinson added: "Anyway, Communism isn't outlawed in the U. S. If Mr. Robeson wants to believe in Communism, that's his right. I prefer not to." Robinson sighed.

"Anything progressive is called Communism."

confidently honor partisans of a cause that once made them targets of wholesale government repression.

Yet even a quarter century later, when it would appear that communism is dead and gone, it is impermissible to speak of it without all sorts of qualifiers and disclaimers. This is a ritual and a loyalty oath we've all witnessed or enacted without realizing, perhaps, the contradiction it presents. At the very moment independent thought and unfettered inquiry are being upheld they are restricted within predetermined limits. It is as if the word "communism" still has the power to put you in the witness box at a HUAC hearing to be grilled by Richard Nixon![2] In short, adopt the requisite anticommunism and you will be permitted to discuss it, otherwise you are anathema.

It is inconceivable that, once upon a time, millions of ordinary workers actually debated the question seriously and without prejudice. It is impossible to reconcile anticommunism with the views expressed in 1937 by black coal miner Angelo Herndon:

> The bosses, and the Negro misleaders like Oscar Adams, told us that these Reds were "foreigners" and "strangers" and that the Communist program wasn't acceptable to the workers in the South. I couldn't see that at all. The leaders of the Communist Party and the Unemployment Council seemed people very much like the ones I'd always been used to. They were workers, and they talked our language. Their talk sure sounded better to me than the talk of Oscar Adams, or the President of the Tennessee Coal, Iron and Railroad Co. who addressed us every once in a while. As for the program not being acceptable to us—I felt then, and I know now, that the Communist program is the only program that the Southern workers—whites and Negroes both—can possibly accept in the long run. It's the only program that does justice to the Southern worker's ideas that everybody ought to have an equal chance, and that every man has rights that must be respected.[3]

---

2   HUAC: House Un-American Activities Committee, an investigative committee of the U.S. House of Representatives created in 1938 to investigate disloyalty and subversive activities. Its purpose was to intimidate. It did in fact threaten the livelihoods of many artists and intellectuals including Pete Seeger, who was convicted of contempt of Congress and later freed on a technicality. Its reign was successfully challenged by a mass protest at its hearings in San Francisco in 1960. From that time forward HUAC was thoroughly discredited. It was finally disbanded in 1975, a year after Richard Nixon resigned the presidency. Nixon had established his reputation by serving on HUAC as a congressman.

3   http://www.historyisaweapon.com/defcon1/herndoncannotkill.html.

"You Cannot Kill the Working Class" by Angelo Herndon

The cover of Herndon's pamphlet co-published in 1937 by the International Labor Defense and the League of Struggle for Negro Rights. https://www.marxists.org/history/usa/pubs/labordefender/pamphlets/You-Cannot-Kill-the-Working-Class-herndon.pdf

Herndon was arrested in Georgia, convicted of insurrection according to an arcane slavery-era statute for leading a peace march and was sentenced to twenty years on a chain gang. His case was taken up by the ILD (see below). Herndon gained international renown, eventually being freed when the U.S. Supreme Court found the law that convicted him to be unconstitutional.

Among the songs in this collection are those written by people who openly embraced communist ideals and joined efforts led by communist militants. This presents both logical contradictions in anticommunist dogma and factual evidence refuting anticommunism's most basic claims. Some may find it embarrassing to admit, but in their own struggle to better their lives, workers grasped the communist idea better than many intellectuals. They furthermore saw dedicated, self-sacrificing representatives of this idea fighting and dying at their side.

The story behind Ella May's song "Toiling On Life's Pilgrim Pathway" is a case in point. The chorus, "Come and join the ILD," refers to the International Labor Defense, an organization of which Ella May was herself a member. A quick Wikipedia search provides the outlines: "The International Labor Defense (ILD) was a legal advocacy organization established in 1925 in the United States as the American section of the Comintern's International Red Aid network. The ILD defended Sacco and Vanzetti, was active in the antilynching movement and the civil rights movement, and prominently participated in the defense and legal appeals in the cause célèbre of the Scottsboro Boys in the early 1930s. Its work contributed to the appeal of the Communist Party among African Americans in the South. In addition to fundraising for defense and assisting in defense strategies, from January 1926 it published the *Labor Defender*, a monthly illustrated magazine that achieved wide circulation."

Reading the *Labor Defender* is quite an eye-opener. Not only does it document countless battles in many parts of the United States and the world, it *demystifies* the period, making clear what was at stake. It's no wonder, as Denning writes, "the propertied classes genuinely feared insurrection and revolution, and young radicals envisioned a Soviet America." It's also no wonder why this episode in American history and its expression in culture needs to be hidden. How could it be that in the Land of the Free and the Home of the Brave there were any so disloyal as to imagine a world without war, poverty, and oppression?

Cover of the *Labor Defender* featuring Ada Wright, the mother of Roy and Andy, two of the Scottsboro boys.

Outside Agitators

Even those who've rejected anticommunist hysteria still often uncritically accept the view that workers are content with their lot and that foreigners with strange names are responsible for stirring them up. The fact that this is a well-known tactic of employers and politicians attempting to isolate workers from each other and their

• • • SCOTTSBORO • • •

BECAUSE the International Labor Defense has exposed the colossal frame-up against the nine Negro boys, showing it to be another Sacco and Vanzetti case on a larger scale,

Because millions of workers, black and white, throughout the United States have demanded the unconditional and immediate release of these nine innocent Negro boys,

Because more millions of workers throughout the European countries have raised their voices of protest against the legal lynching of these Scottsboro Negro boys,

THE HAND OF DEATH HAS BEEN STAYED!

The electric chair has thus far been denied its victims.

The United States Supreme Court will review and pass upon the I.L.D. demand for a new trial of the nine Scottsboro Negro boys.

On October 10th, next, in Washington, D. C., the last legal move against the sentence of these boys rendered by the State of Alabama, will be enacted.

The murderous capitalist class has the stage all set—their actors are well paid, their henchmen and perjurers have received their price.

With the prosecution money is no object.

BUT the International Labor Defense upon whose shoulders rests the responsibility to raise the enormous legal cost of the defense, stands with its back against the wall—with its sleeves rolled up, working day and night to raise the necessary sum of over $5,000 which must be paid before the date set for the hearing. October 10th, next.

WORKERS AND FRIENDS:

Without your help this task cannot be performed. The I.L.D is your machinery of defense. It is upon you, the victims depend Only mass pressure, only your financial aid, will bring freedom to the nine Scottsboro Negro victims.

Remember October 10th. Act now — today! Give all you can. Get every friend to do the same. Collect everywhere.

TO THE I.L.D. SCOTTSBORO DEFENSE
80 East 11th Street, New York, N. Y.

Comrades :

Enclosed please find (my) (our) donation of............
for the defense of the nine innocent Scottsboro Negro boys.

....(Signed)

....(Address)

supporters does not automatically reduce its effectiveness. Partly, this is because the "outside agitator" is subtly implied, rather than explicitly invoked, in contexts other than workplace actions or political movements. The prime example is found in the marketing strategies of the music industry, where "hillbilly," "race," and other labels, identified who was in and who was out of a given "community" or social stratum. But this was not simply packaging products to fit already-existing social distinctions. It was reinforcing divisions and creating new ones. Publicists for the music industry were not only selling what was profitable but were purging the music they were selling of any subversive content. Any reference to class struggle or political revolution was systematically excluded.

When Aunt Molly Jackson sang, "I was raised in old Kentucky, Kentucky borned and bred, and when I joined the union, they called me a Rooshian Red," she knew what she was singing about. She ridiculed the charge at the same time she defied those making it. Obviously, coal miners knew this, as well. Furthermore, they knew what lay behind the charge: a revolution their enemies hated and feared. It should come as no surprise that an attack on Ella May Wiggins and her comrades in the Textile Workers Union was led by a mob chanting, "We're all 100 percent Americans and anybody that don't like it can go back to Russia . . . Long live 100% Americanism!"

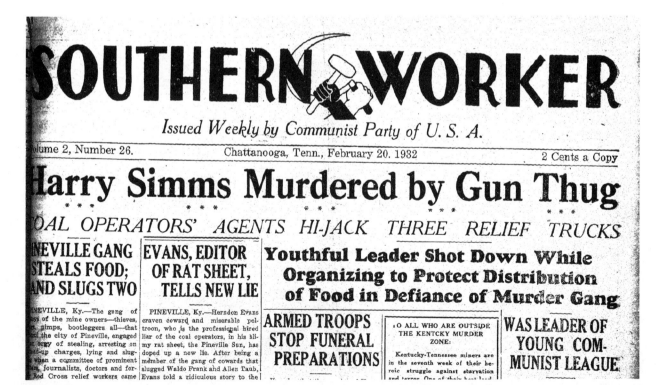

The murder of Harry Simms and Jim Garland's song of that name concentrate all the foregoing in one powerful example. Harry Simms, as the song says, was killed on Brush Creek, Kentucky, in 1932. He was the typical outside agitator having been born in Springfield, Massachusetts, only coming to the South to organize, first in Birmingham, Alabama, and later in Kentucky. But what was Harry Simms outside of? He was not outside the working class. His parents were workers, and he went to work in a textile mill at the age of fourteen. He spent four months in jail after being arrested at a demonstration of the unemployed. Upon joining the Young Communist League, Harry headed south to support the Sharecroppers Union in Birmingham. He fought the frame-up of a black miner, Willie Peterson, campaigned for the Scottsboro Boys, and aided in the battle of sharecroppers at Camp Hill.[4] When he moved to

4   The Scottsboro Boys case involved nine young African Americans accused of raping a white woman in 1931. They were convicted and sentenced to death. Their defense, led by the CPUSA and the NAACP, grew into an international movement, exposing Jim Crow, white supremacy, and the role of government in maintaining an unjust social order.

      Camp Hill, Alabama, was the site of a major confrontation between the Sharecroppers Union and a white mob in 1931. A union member was murdered, others were injured, and thirty were arrested. A campaign was launched which led to those in custody being released without trial.

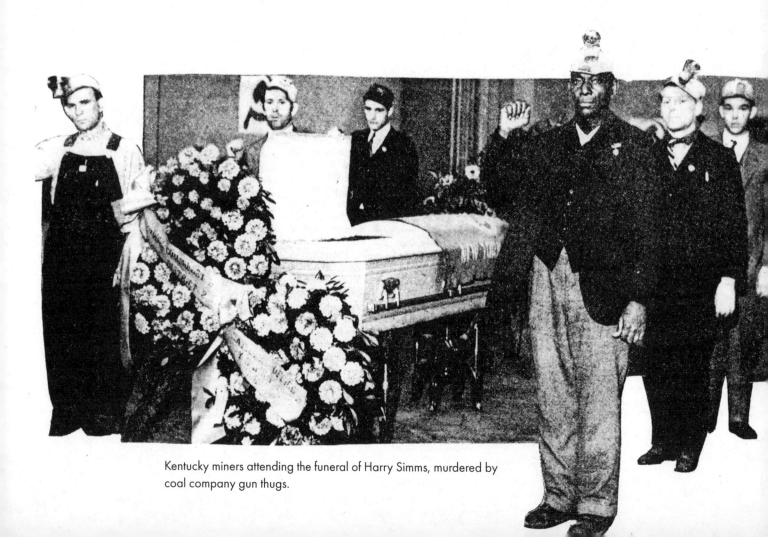

Kentucky miners attending the funeral of Harry Simms, murdered by coal company gun thugs.

Kentucky to organize relief for the striking miners, he was immediately befriended by miner Jim Garland. Jim loved Harry like a brother, and every line in the song is true. So we're forced to decide. Either these people were all dupes and fools or they were among the bravest and most committed fighters the working class has produced.

The Commonwealth of Toil

The core premise of this project is that workers will struggle to improve their conditions of life. Among them will be workers who share an insight: in order to better our lot, we must act collectively to change the *world*. The songs here prove that this premise is true. It follows, therefore, that our best hope lies in the capacity of ordinary working people to awaken to the need to emancipate themselves and all humanity and to act accordingly.

Sustaining this hope, however, requires more than the courage and determination to fight. Courage and determination need the nourishment of the "glowing dream" that inspired Ralph Chaplin's great song "The Commonwealth of Toil." This dream is as much a part of the present as of the future it foretells. Here and now, the vision of a world transformed is a guide as well as a destination, a star in the heavens that will not be dimmed. At every turn it is met by cynical disdain and violent repression. Yet this vision has sustained the downtrodden for millennia and it will remain a beacon until its promise has been fulfilled.

The Miners of Kentucky Call You !

*Five of the strike leaders in jail.
Free them.*

*Two of these imprisoned women leaders
face lynching in Harlan prison.*

In Kentucky, workers are being plugged with bullets, beaten till they can't stand up, and have to crawl home, or jailed in "the rocks," where the rats keep them awake all night. These workers are striking against starvation wages.

In Kentucky, it is a crime punishable by death, to be a striker. In Kentucky, the miners say, if you're "hongry," they call you a *Red*; and if you talke about it, you're a criminal syndicalist. In Kentucky, the miners say again, if you stand your ground, they shoot you in the stomach; if you try to get away, they shoot you in the back.

All along the Kentucky front the Terror is spreading like a prairie fire. This same Terror is sweeping the country; it has flared up in Chicago, Detroit, Tampa. But it is most brazen in Kentucky. *There*, instructions have been given gun thugs to shoot at sight. There, nineteen strike leaders have been put in jail since January first. Each faces trial before a framed jury for 21 years in the penitentiary.

The International Labor Defense is fighting for their freedom. It cannot carry on its fight without funds. The desperate struggle of miners striking for life is your struggle. Every dollar you give is like a bucket of water thrown on this fire of Terror that is spreading everywhere. Get these organizers out of prison! They are your leaders! They are trying to save YOU from what is happening to the Kentucky miners.

Rush funds to:

INTERNATIONAL LABOR DEFENSE
80 East Eleventh Street, Room 430
NEW YORK CITY

SINGERS, SONGS, AND HEROES

BIOGRAPHICAL SKETCHES

Ella May Wiggins

(September 17, 1900, Sevierville, Tennessee–September 14, 1929, Gastonia, North Carolina)

Ella May Wiggins was a union organizer and balladeer who was murdered during the Loray Mill Strike in Gastonia, North Carolina. At the time, the Loray Mill was the largest of its kind in the world, and the mill owners had already violently attacked the strike. She was driving to a union meeting in Gastonia with fellow union members when an armed mob confronted them. They turned back. After driving about five miles, a car blocked their path, and several men got out and started shooting at them. Wiggins, shot in the chest, was killed. She was survived by five children, who were sent to orphanages.

Her great-granddaughter, Kristina Horton, published a biography in 2015, *Martyr of Loray Mill*. Horton said in an interview: "When Communist labor organizers came south to the Loray

Working for the union and I am also Doing all I can for the I L D - and I will Continue untill it is through and if you are a worker we want you to for we are going to Have a union inspite of what The Boss Says

a striker Ella May - Bessemer city

What I Believe

By ELLA MAY

Ella May

The following article was written by Ella May on the back of a National Textile Workers' Union leaflet the day after the Manville-Jenckes Black Hundred had raided I. L. D. and Union headquarters in Gastonia and Charlotte and kidnapped Ben Wells, Saylors and Lell, Union organizers. It was written but a few days before Ella May was killed by a Manville-Jenckes murderer. She had probably intended to send it to one of the papers. It was found among her belongings after her death.—EDITOR.

I THINK that the mill owners see they cannot send our leaders and our other boys to the chair, and last night they made a raid on the headquarters in Gastonia and also Bessemer City. I think they thought it would scare all the workers down here and they would quit the union.

But what buts them is that it only makes us stronger. If I had not already belonged I would join now. But I joined when it first came down here and I am not ashamed of it. I can't speak to do any good, but I try. And I do anything else I can to benefit myself and other workers. And if every one of the workers could see it as I can, we would have no trouble winning, and I hope whoever was in that mob of thugs last night will have to suffer. But we cannot look for the law to punish their own bunch.

We must still stick out for our rights. That is what will whip the mill-owners and they see we are going to win out. I want every worker to stick together, and if we do we are sure to win, and if we don't stand up for our rights and we hang on the bosses, we are fighting ourselves and fighting our children and against our freedom for the working class.

Down here in the South we have never had any freedom since I can remember and I am now 29 years old and I have got five children of my own and I want them to have something to want to live for and not have to slave all their days away for nothing, like I have had to do.

When I came out on strike I was only making eight or nine dollars a week and working 11 hours at night. I mean I worked. I did not stop from the time I went in till I came out and I want to say ever since I came out of the American mill on the night of the strike, I have

been working for the Union and I am also doing all I can for the I. L. D. and I will continue until it is through.

If you are a worker we want you, for we are going to have a union inspite of what the boss says.

To All Comrades

COMRADES, we the people of the South, have been slaves for the bosses long enough. Now, since April 1, we have been awakening and seeing where we have been and what we are doing. We have opened our eyes wide enough to see that we are not people but slaves for the bosses. The long hours we have been slaving away, nearing our graves, have been making the bosses richer.

This is just because the bosses never let the people know anything about strikes, and in school the teacher never says anything about how we slave, and are always giving parties or some sports to keep the workers' minds off the hard work they have done in the week, night or day. So, in this way, the workers never have time

to think. Now the workers of the North have seen what we were doing and are trying to help us better our conditions.

Since I have been in the North I have learned more about what we were doing. I saw the children from Russia, where workers are free, and have heard what is going on.

Now I am more determined to go back South and organize the older workers and children, regardles of boss, police or anything.

Always for the workers,
Comradely yours,
BINNIE GREEN.
(14-year old Gastonia mill striker)

Mill, Ella May joined right away. She was a secretary for the Union. As the strike progressed, she took a more vocal role. . . . The last year of Ella May's life was an extremely violent time. The spring [the family] received their water from was poisoned; Myrtle, Ella May's eldest child, was raped when she was 11 in front of her sisters and brothers."

Commenting specifically on May's organizing of black mill workers at the height of Jim Crow, Horton said: "There were no airs about her. Most whites living in the Piedmont at the time thought of themselves as superior to black workers. But Ella May didn't grow up in a place where there was much prejudice or even classes. She carried that heritage with her. She saw black workers as her equals. When she'd go to Union meetings, there'd be a rope dividing whites and blacks. She was the only white person who would go across to the other side. And honestly, she was as poor as them. She lived in a black mill community. She suffered alongside of them. She knew what they were going through, because she was going through it too."

Before a congressional committee investigating the conflict in Gastonia, Ella May testified: "I'm the mother of nine. Four died with the whooping cough, all at once. I was working nights, I asked the super to put me on days, so's I could tend 'em when they had their bad spells. But he wouldn't. I don't know why. . . . So I had to quit, and then there wasn't no money for medicine, and they just died."

Shortly before her death Ella May wrote, "I want every worker to stick together, and if we do we are sure to win, and if we don't stand up for our rights and we hang on the bosses, we are fighting ourselves and fighting our children and against our freedom for the working class."

Aunt Molly Jackson
(1880, Clay County, Kentucky–September 1, 1960, Sacramento, California)

"America's Hundred Years' War was fought in the coal fields," wrote John Greenway in *American Folksongs of Protest*. "Since 1849, when an English Chartist named John Bates formed in Pennsylvania's Schuylkill County the first American miners' union, there have been hundreds of battles in this continuous struggle, and 'battle' is not a figure of speech." Miners' struggles spanned the North American continent from Appalachia, to Michigan, to Colorado, each region remembered by the sites of open warfare between workers and capitalists, the latter supported by police and federal troops. Ludlow, Colorado; Calumet, Michigan; and Harlan County, Kentucky, were at various times the flashpoints of class struggle in the United States.

I Am from Kentucky Born

By AUNT MOLLY JACKSON

Aunt Molly, who puts into songs the sufferings of her people. "Bound Down in Prison" is her song.

Three more Harlan Miners are facing murder charges in Harlan, Kentucky.

Virgil Hutton, Kike Hall, and Leonard Farmer, active members of the National Miners Union, were arrested for shooting Deputy Sheriff Virgil Sizemore, December 25. They were distributing N. M. U. leaflets calling for a general strike on January 1 when a band of drunken thugs attacked them. Hutton's head was split open. One sheriff's gunman was killed.

The International Labor Defense sees in this new instance of terror Sheriff Blair's plan to crush the National Miners Union and cripple the strike. The attack on Hutton, Hall and Farmer, and the murder charges brought against them will also be used by the coal company courts to influence the jury against William Hightower, miner from Evarts, who went on trial Dec. 8 at Mt. Sterling.

I AM from Kentucky. Borned and raised in the Kentucky coal fields. I know all about just how the coal miners and their famleys have ben treated by coal operators from the time I was old enuf to remember till this date. I will tell you a few sad storeys that has befell the coal miners in the last few weeks.

One is this. One of my own dear brothers was taken from his wife and three small children and placed in the county jail in Pineville, Bell County, Ky., charged with criminal syncalism when he sertenley was not guilty. The miners at Glendon mines and Straight Creek came out on strike on a count of the operator refusing to let them have a checkwayman to way their coal. My brother and seven of the other miners went to the operator and ask him to allow them a checkwayman and this made the operator so mad that he had my brother, W. M. Garland and seven other miners arrested and took them and put them in jail and would not allow them any bonds for six days. Then allowed them to fill bonds amounting to six thousand dollars each.

My brother and five other miners have filed bonds and one poor coal miner by the name of Ebbe Payne is still in jail.

Payne has a wife and six children needing his seport. Payne's wife came to me and told me her children were starving and that the operators had framed up a lot of lyes on her husband and had tuck him an' put him behind the coald iron bars and her children were suffering all most death from hunger and coald.

Dear comrades, I have had a lot of heart rendering things happen to me. The next I shall tell you is this. On the same night after I had ben working all day long trying to get bond for my friend Payne, I had just got home and droped down in a chair an' said to my husband, "Oh, my god, I am all most tired to death," when some one rapped on my shack door and it was my own dear baby-brother running away from the deputy sherif and gun thugs to keep from bein' tuck to jail for criminal synaclism when he was not gilty. But he knew he would be put in if they caught him. So J. C. Garland, my youngest brother, left his loving wife and four heart broken sisters and a dear loveing mother and two other brothers, to weep over his departure.

Not long a go a man an his wife were cooking at a soup house of the National Miners an the gun thugs came in an said, "The coal operator sent us down here to kill your husband an blow up this soup kitchen so if you want to save your life an' your three children's life, beat it, we're going to kill your husband and dinamite hell out of this National Miners Union kitchen."

Just after they had said this to the

BOUND DOWN IN PRISON

It is sad to be bound down in prison,
In a cold prison cell all alone,
With the cold iron bars all around me
And my head on a pillow of stone.

The coal operators and the bosses
Had me placed in this cold lonely jail;
I heard them tell the jailer this morning
They never would allow me any bail.

The coal operators and the bosses
Want to keep me in prison all my life,
But there is no use to count on losses,
I want you to take this letter to my wife.

I want her to know I am in prison,
Just as lonely as a poor man can be;
Go tell her to write me a letter
And send it to the dear old I.L.D.

This I.L.D. works for prisoners,
And I know they will work wonders for me;
Write and tell them I'm a Harlan County prisoner
Depending on the dear old I.L.D.

poor union miner's wife these gun thugs shot the poor woman's husban down dead by her side. Then the woman grabbed her baby up and ron away and the other two children after her.

So let us all unite together and fight starvation, wage cuts. Uniting is what it takes to win our libberty an freedom.

I remain your true friend and faithful worker. —AUNT MOLLIE JACKSON.

Aunt Molly Jackson was born Mary Magdalene Garland into a mining family; her father, Oliver Garland, a miner, organizer, and ordained Baptist minister. She got her nickname "Aunt Molly" because she was a midwife, delivering hundreds of babies in her time. She got the name Jackson from her second husband, Bill Jackson. According to historian John Hevener, "When Jackson was jailed because of her unionizing activities, her husband was forced to divorce her in order to keep his mining job." By that time, however, Aunt Molly Jackson had become so well known that her name was a symbol of working-class resistance. It would follow her to her grave.

In 1931, the National Miners Union spearheaded the latest attempt to establish an effective organization in coal country. The NMU was part of the Communist Party's national strategy to organize industries, especially in the South, that had been abandoned by the unions of the American Federation of Labor. This effort met with the usual violent reprisals but with added emphasis on anticommunist "God and Country" propaganda. The entire Garland family would eventually be involved in the struggle and all would be branded and persecuted as a result. When national attention was drawn to the Harlan County War, Aunt Molly testified before a committee headed by writer Theodore Dreiser, which had come to investigate. She sang her composition "Ragged, Hungry Blues" for the committee and soon thereafter was invited to New York City to help raise funds for the striking miners. She would settle there and become involved in the political whirlwind of Depression-era New York. Aunt Molly would become friends with Leadbelly, Charles Seeger and the Composers' Collective, Woody Guthrie, Pete Seeger, and a host of writers and artists involved with the Communist Party. She would eventually record over two hundred songs, one a commercial single, and was for many years active politically, singing, speaking, and raising funds for various causes.

Jim Garland
(April 8, 1905, Fourmile, Kentucky–September 6, 1978, Washougal, Washington)

A coal miner, union organizer, brother of Sarah Ogan Gunning, and half brother of Aunt Molly Jackson, Jim Garland might be the best remembered of the Garland family due to his song "I Don't Want Your Millions, Mister," which became a staple of the folk music revival of the 1960s. Initially, however, Garland, was a union organizer, devoted to the National Miners Union and a special target of the coal operators. Indeed, it was Garland's firm belief that the bullet that killed Harry Simms was meant for him. At the height of that battle, Garland would travel to New York to join Aunt Molly in

Jim Garland from Pete Seeger's personal collection; photographer unknown.

fundraising for the striking miners and to the memorial for Harry Simms, attended by more than twenty thousand people. Not long after, the NMU was crushed, and Garland was effectively driven out of the coal fields—blacklisted, threatened, and impoverished. He would end up in New York to join Aunt Molly and to be joined later by Sarah and her dying husband, Andrew Ogan. During World War II, Garland moved his family to Vancouver, Washington, to find work in the shipyards.

Garland continued writing and performing music well into the 1960s, befriending many of those who would gain far greater renown popularizing his songs than he ever did. Like others in his family and the wider circle associated with the labor movement, the Communist Party, and American folk music, it was the latter category—American folk music—that became a safe haven, especially during the anticommunist hysteria of the McCarthy period. Contradictory trends—expanding popularity of folk music and brutal suppression of communism—mark the life and work of many musicians and folklorists, including, of course, Pete Seeger, Woody Guthrie, and Alan Lomax.

Near the end of his life, Garland turned over a wealth of recordings to Folkways Records that are now in the Ralph Rinzler Folklife Archives and Collections of the Smithsonian Center for Folklife and Cultural Heritage. He also completed his autobiography, *Welcome the Traveler Home*. Garland wrote a song with that title many years before, as he was preparing to return to Kentucky from New York. It says a great deal about the hardships he faced and the spirit with which he faced them. The first and concluding stanzas read:

For to welcome the traveler home
For to welcome the traveler home
The gun thugs they are waiting
To welcome the traveler home

When I get back to Kentucky.
And I get my .45's on,
They'll be another Boston Tea Party
If they try to welcome this red-neck home.

We Blame Rockefeller and Morgan

Harry Simms, 19-year-old organizer for the National Miners Union, was murdered by a thug of the southeastern Kentucky coal companies. These mines are owned by Morgan and Rockefeller interests. The death of Simms is the fault of the multi-millionaires. Workers through out America are holding protest meetings; rushing wires of protest against the terror in Kentucky to the governor of that state; swearing to avenge his death by building a stronger workers' movement for which Simms gave his life.

The mines in Ky. are controlled by Rockefeller and Morgan interests. Their gunmen killed 19-year-old Harry Simms.

LABOR DEFENDER

OCT 9 '32

MARCH
1932

10¢

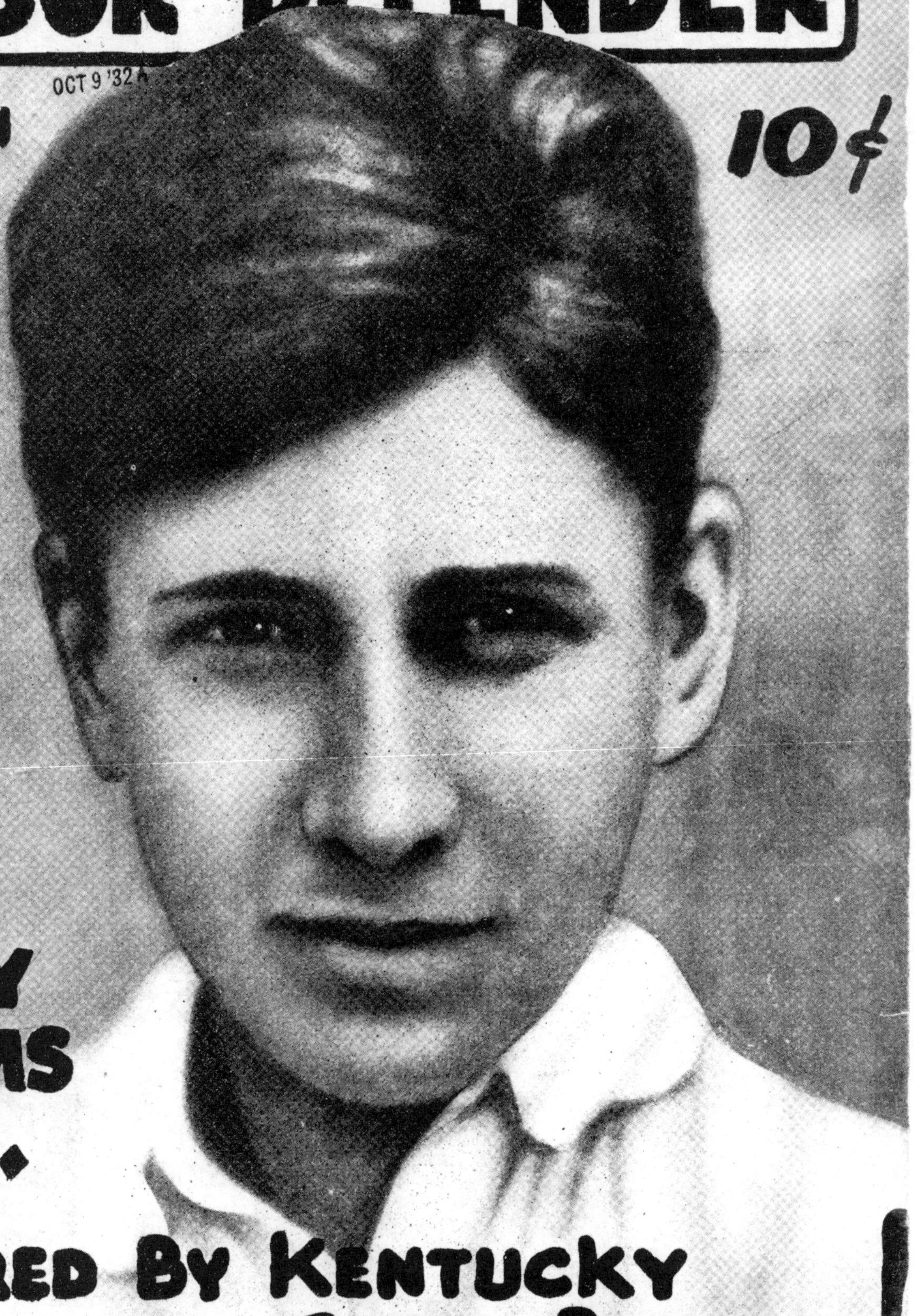

HARRY
SIMMS
·19·
MURDERED BY KENTUCKY
COAL BOSSES!

In this Issue
Tom Lo De W

Sarah Ogan Gunning

(June 28, 1910, Elys Branch, Knox County, Kentucky–November 14, 1983, Knoxville, Tennessee; her last home was in Hart, Michigan, but she died while attending a family gathering.)

Sarah Elizabeth Garland was born in the coal camps, sharing the fate of her siblings and other mining families. This included early marriage (at age fifteen), to miner Andrew Ogan, and motherhood of four children, two of whom died in infancy for lack of proper nutrition. Her husband would later succumb to TB undoubtedly related to silicosis, or "black lung," contracted in the mines. Sarah was also surrounded by militant resistance to such conditions, as her father, husband, and brother Jim were active in attempts to organize the miners. Like her half sister Aunt Molly Jackson and her brother Jim Garland, Sarah would eventually move to New York and join in efforts to support the miners in Kentucky. She wrote many of her songs there in the early 1930s to aid in that work. Embraced by like-minded musicians, writers, and organizers, Sarah was often asked to contribute songs at public and private gatherings. This led, in 1937, to her being recorded, first by Alan Lomax and then by Mary Elizabeth Barnicle. The recordings are in the Library of Congress.

After her first husband died, Sarah married Joseph Gunning. During the war, the Gunnings moved to Vancouver, Washington, to work in the shipyards. After the war they moved to Detroit for work in the auto industry. She was later "discovered" by folklorist Archie Green and extensively interviewed by Green and two academic colleagues, Ellen Stekert and Oscar Paskal from Wayne State University. They arranged to record Sarah's album, *Girl of Constant Sorrow*, in 1964. Later that year she would appear at the Newport Folk Festival, an appearance that led to more invitations and more festival appearances in the years to come. A good film was made, some essays were written, a chapter in a book was devoted to her life. Sarah thus enjoyed a few years of popular appreciation, presumably deriving some satisfaction from the warm reception she received. Soon enough, however, Sarah Ogan Gunning was again forgotten.

Her brief and belated notoriety highlights the fact that, with the exception of Paul Robeson, none of the singers in this collection were professionals, nor were they pursuing careers when they wrote and performed their songs. That Gunning received a bit of recognition late in life might be viewed as some small compensation or reward. But such recognition should not obscure the cause her songs were written to serve. The dilemma facing the folk music revival, and even the publication of books such as

Hard Hitting Songs, was that changing circumstances notwithstanding, the workers' struggle goes on. In the 1960s and '70s, in fact, there were numerous strikes by coal miners. But by this time folk music was both well-established as entertainment and far removed from workers and their struggles. The greatest honor we can bestow upon Sarah Ogan Gunning is to have her songs serve the struggle of workers today.

Sarah Ogan Gunning and Pete Seeger. © Jim Marshall Photography LLC

John L. Handcox
(Brinkley, Arkansas, February 5, 1904–San Diego, California, September 18, 1992)

The Great Depression, the Dust Bowl, and the migration of Okies and Arkies to California, have been mythologized in Steinbeck's *Grapes of Wrath*, the photographs of Dorothea Lange, and the songs and persona of Woody Guthrie. Missing in this near-biblical image of exodus and redemption is the struggle of the tenant farmers of the South. Central to this struggle were organizations that defied the old white plantation oligarchy whose power had not been diminished by defeat in the Civil War. In Alabama the Share Croppers Union and in Arkansas (and several other states) the Southern Tenant Farmers Union (STFU) led the battle to limit hours of work, increase pay, prevent eviction, and allow personal cultivation of food, among other demands. Due to the collapse in farm prices and efforts of the federal government to reduce acreage under cultivation, John Handcox and his family were faced, like so many others, with utter destitution. But Handcox chose to fight rather than to flee. When the STFU came to Arkansas, Handcox joined and quickly became one of the union's most effective organizers, in no small part due to his songwriting and singing. In 1935 a great strike was organized. Handcox explained:

> In the spring, at cotton chopping time, it didn't make much difference if we was working or not—our young ones was still hungry. So we began to talk about a strike. Most of us was workin' from sun up to sun down for less than 70 cents a day. We wanted $1.50 a day for ten hours work. We made handbills and posters and signs telling what we wanted and plastered them up all over the place. There were about four thousand altogether who said they would go on strike.
>
> The planters got scared. The laws arrested every man they could git hold of and took them back to work at the point of guns. They beat up men and women and shot some and tried to scare us. They ran a lot of folks out. But they couldn't break the strike. We had marches. We all lined up, sometimes more than a hundred of us on a line, and marched through the plantations and cross country. In lots of places where we marched the choppers stopped work and went on strike with us. At one plantation the scabs they had brought from other places dropped their hoes and run like rabbits when they saw us comin'.

At its height, the STFU had thirty thousand members in Arkansas, Missouri, Oklahoma, and Texas. It led one great strike (described above), sent members to lobby

John Handcox, from Pete Seeger's personal collection; photographer unknown.

Congress, and was successful throughout its brief, violent history, in maintaining solidarity in an openly interracial union. Employed by the union as an organizer, Handcox traveled extensively in the Midwest and Northeast using his songs to raise funds and awareness. In Washington, DC, he was recorded by Charles Seeger and Sidney Robertson for the Library of Congress in 1937. But planter repression ultimately destroyed the union, and Handcox was blacklisted, threatened with lynching, and driven from Arkansas. In 1942 he'd joined the great wartime migration out of the South, finding work as a carpenter in San Diego. He then "disappeared" for the next forty years.

Even though he wasn't there, Handcox's songs continued to be widely sung and were already folk music standards by the time *Hard Hitting Songs* was published. "Roll The Union On," "No More Mournin'" and "Mean Things Happening In This Land" are among the best known. Pete Seeger recalls searching for Handcox: "A full thirty-five years later we connected." Seeger then arranged to have Handcox perform at various folk festivals and union gatherings.

Handcox remained a fighter to the end, composing songs critical of Reagan in 1984. In an interview given to the *Los Angeles Times* in 1985 he expressed his motive for songwriting: "Life is not a matter of money with me. If my songs help make this a better world to live in, I think I did a lot."

Joe Hill

(October 7, 1879, Gävle, Sweden–November 19, 1915, Salt Lake City, Utah; born Joel Emmanuel Hägglund and also known as Joseph Hillström)

Hill immigrated to the United States in 1902, traveling widely and frequently within the country as an itinerant laborer. He joined the Industrial Workers of the World (IWW) around 1910. Hill's mythical status is built on a foundation of songs he composed, activism in the IWW, and, of course, his frame-up and execution by the authorities in Salt Lake City. At the time of his arrest, Hill was already well known. His songs had been popularized as the struggles led by the Wobblies and the Western Federation of Miners made international headlines. Songs such as "The Preacher And The Slave," "The Rebel Girl," "There Is Power In A Union," and "Casey Jones—The Union Scab," were sung throughout the U.S. and have subsequently been immortalized in many song books. In a telegram sent to IWW leader Bill Haywood shortly before his execution, Hill wrote: "Goodbye, Bill: I die like a true blue rebel. Don't waste any time mourning. Organize!" Hill then concluded

Watercolor portrait of Joe Hill by Ralph Chaplin.

with his customary humor: "Could you arrange to have my body hauled to the state line to be buried? I don't want to be found dead in Utah."

Ralph Hosea Chaplin
(1887, Ames, Kansas–1961, Tacoma, Washington)

Chaplin was a militant labor leader, songwriter, and illustrator famous for composing "Solidarity Forever." Lesser known is his involvement with Mother Jones in the West Virginia coal strikes of 1912–13 and his imprisonment for four years under the Espionage Act of 1917. In the latter case, Chaplin was rounded up with more than a hundred other Wobblies for opposing U.S. entry into World War I. The IWW motto—"Capitalists of America, we will fight against you, not for you!"—expressed a viewpoint shared by many in the labor movement at the time, leading to massive government repression.

Chaplin's work as an illustrator was as celebrated as the songs he composed, for example, the black cat, made famous by the Wobblies as a symbol of the "wildcat" strike, is said to be his work. Chaplin published his first collection of songs, *When the Leaves Come Out and Other Rebel Verses*, in 1917. Following his release from prison Chaplin published *Bars and Shadows: The Prison Poems*. The introduction, written by well-known radical economist Scott Nearing, summed up a great deal about Chaplin's life and times:

> As a member of the Industrial Workers of the World, Ralph Chaplin did his part
> to make the organization a success. He wrote songs and poems; he made speeches:
> he edited the official paper, *Solidarity*. He looked about him; saw poverty, wretch-

edness and suffering among the workers; contrasted it with the luxury of those who owned the land and the machinery of production; studied the problem of distribution; and decided that it was possible, through the organization of the producers, to establish a more scientific, juster, more humane system of society. All this he felt, intensely. With him and his fellow-workers the task of freeing humanity from economic bondage took on the aspect of a faith, a religion. They held their meetings; wrote their literature; made their speeches and sang their songs with zealous devotion. They had seen a vision; they had heard a call to duty; they were giving their lives to a cause—the emancipation of the human race.

Paul Robeson

(April 9, 1898, Princeton, New Jersey–January 23, 1976, Philadelphia, Pennsylvania)

One might expect that given his prodigious talents and international stardom, Paul Robeson's life would be promoted as a "success story," proof that in the Land of the Free, even the son of a slave could fulfill his dreams and achieve greatness. But this overlooks the fact that even though he was a great singer, actor, athlete, and intellectual, Robeson was above all a champion of workers and oppressed people. His internationalist and communist sympathies placed him squarely in the sites of the U.S. government, and Robeson spent most of his adult life fighting against efforts to silence him. Blacklists and McCarthy hearings, travel bans and canceled performances, physical attacks and psychological intimidation made Robeson's life a continuous battle.

Illustration of Paul Robeson by Charles Henry Alston, 1907-1977, (NARA record: 3569253). https://en.wikipedia.org/wiki/Charles_Alston.

Indeed, it is a wonder that Robeson accomplished so much in so many fields of endeavor given the obstacles thrown in his path. Clearly, the love and respect he received from workers the world over sustained him. Near the end of his life he recorded a message: "Though I have not been able to be active for several years, I want you to know that I am the same Paul, dedicated as ever to the worldwide cause of humanity for freedom, peace and brotherhood."

Fortunately, many recordings of his majestic voice are readily available as are the films in which he performed. Furthermore, Robeson's achievements have finally, albeit belatedly, gained a portion of the recognition they deserve. Yet, even today, his uncompromising stand on questions such as loyalty to the United States and support for the Soviet Union, prevent his complete rehabilitation by the liberal establishment. He may be on a postage stamp, there may be schools named after him, but no one has held the FBI or Congress accountable for the persecution they orchestrated while he was alive. No one in the entertainment industry will soon be acknowledging their complicity in this shameful episode, either. None of these institutions will ever celebrate the cause that imbued Robeson's life with such nobility of purpose. As he wrote in his autobiography, *Here I Stand*: "A socialist society represents an advance to a higher stage of life—that is, a form of society which is economically, socially, culturally, and ethically superior to a system based upon production for private profit. History shows that the processes of social change have nothing in common with silly notions about 'plots' and 'conspiracies.' The development of human society—from tribalism to feudalism, to capitalism, to socialism—is brought about by the needs and aspirations of mankind for a better life." Because he would never renounce these ideals and the efforts to realize them, Robeson was punished. But that is also why, like Joe Hill, he will never die.

NOTES ON THE SONGS

BEFORE GOING INTO THE PARTICULARS, A FEW GENERAL POINTS NEED TO BE made. For centuries, the word "song" was used to designate a poem or lyric independent of any particular melody (think of the biblical "Song of Songs"). Subsequently, "song" was used to designate both lyrics *and* melody when the only thing specific or original to the song in question was the lyric. "Which Side Are You On," for example, is a song written by a union organizer's wife, Florence Reese. But the only unique contribution Reese made was the text. The melody came from an old church hymn, "Lay The Lily Low." Another example is Woody Guthrie's best-known song, "This Land Is Your Land." The lyrics are Woody's but the music is "When The World's On Fire," recorded by the Carter Family, which was itself derived from an old Baptist hymn. In fact, the music to most of the songs in our collection has no known author and took recognizable shape long before being used in the manner it is here. Much of the music, like that of "Which Side Are You On," is Christian and was originally composed for and disseminated by various Protestant churches. Other melodies originated in the various functions music has served for thousands of years: working, dancing, marching, courting, and putting babies to bed.

One point, however, must not be missed: the music in this collection came from all over the place, geographically and historically, and was simply put to use by lyricists as they saw fit. Some were old church hymns, others were commercial "hits." Some were first composed and sung by slaves only to be adapted and sung by white congregants. Others began as deliberately written propaganda for either religious or political purposes, to then be parodied by Joe Hill and others. In any case, the only distinguishing characteristic in our collection is one we imposed to prove a point: with one exception, the songs we chose were written by working-class people engaged in struggle, not by professional musicians. (The exception is "Joe Hill" written by Earl Robinson and Alfred Hayes.)

All of which leads to one conclusion: the reason these songs are not included among the great or "classic" tunes in any genre, be it folk, blues, roots, or pop, is because they attack the injustices perpetuated by the system. It cannot be because of any musical deficiency. The music is, after all, the *same* as that of the better-known variety. Thus, by their very existence, these songs expose the hollowness and hypocrisy of "freedom" and "democracy" in America. They furthermore attest to the courage and determination of those who made them.

1. Come All You Coal Miners
words and music: Sarah Ogan Gunning

Yvonne often starts our concerts singing this song without introduction. Not only does it need no explanation, but it immediately commands the attention of the audience with its call, "Come all ye." This may be surprising to those who've never heard music without loud speakers to amplify it. But it won't be to those who recognize the melody's similarity to many Irish and Scottish songs of great antiquity. Not only is the melody similar but it is a common practice for a woman to sing such songs completely unaccompanied, calling on all present to listen. This then recalls a time when, as Gunning herself said, "Everybody nearly in Kentucky sang and made up some songs. Mostly we sang at church. Other times we sang mostly just for our own amusement. Whatever mood we was in we sang. You sang when you washed dishes, you sang when you worked. Even the men folks, they sang. They used to say that if you had a very difficult something to do and it was really hard to do, if you would start a good old spiritual song you could get it done a lot easier." (Interviews given to Archie Green and Ellen Stekert. FT 2785 and FT 2788, respectively. See Sources section below.)

2. There Is Mean Things Happening In This Land
words: John Handcox/additional words Mat Callahan
music: traditional arranged by Mat Callahan and Yvonne Moore

This is one of many songs John Handcox wrote in the course of a long life. We discovered, upon listening to Handcox's own version, that it is actually two songs in one. The first half is a chant combined with a chorus combined with a ballad that tells the story of the strike. The second half follows a regular pattern and it speaks to conditions all workers and farmers face, to this day. In fact, Handcox gives a brilliant summation of capitalist crisis in a few short stanzas. We chose to omit the first half and concentrate on the second because it speaks with such immediacy to our current situation. Musically, we used Handcox's own performance as a guide but put a groove under it to drive the point home.

For more information on the particular strike this song was composed for, please read the biographical note on John Handcox.

The lyrics we omitted are the following:

On the eighteenth day of May
The Union called a strike,
But the planters and the bosses
Throwed the people out of their shacks.

The planters threw the people off the land,
Where many years they'd spent,
And in the hard cold winter,
They had to live in tents.

The planters threw the people out,
Without a bite to eat,
They cursed them and kicked them,
And some with axe handles beat.

The people got tired of working for nothing,
And that from sun to sun,
But the planters forced some to work
At the point of guns.

3. I Am A Girl Of Constant Sorrow

words: Sarah Ogan Gunning

music: traditional

While the original song is usually credited to a blind Kentucky fiddler named Richard Burnett (dated 1913), it is more likely that the melody is much older and the words to what Burnett called "Farewell Song" were his contribution. It became "Man of Constant Sorrow" when Emry Arthur recorded it in 1928, and the name stuck through dozens of different versions. Whatever its origin, Gunning took what she knew was a well-known song and put her own words to it. Apparently she wrote them after she'd arrived in New York City with a husband slowly dying from tuberculosis related to silicosis or "black lung." The lyrics differ from the more commonly known "Man Of Constant Sorrow" in some particulars of the narrative. But the biggest difference is that the latter refers to heaven on "God's golden shore" while Gunning's refers to "Hell on Earth."

4. Come On Friends And Let's Go Down

words: Sarah Ogan Gunning

music: "The Good Ol' Way" (unknown author)

Another of the songs given renewed popularity by *O Brother, Where Art Thou?*, this one was no doubt learned by Gunning as a spiritual. The song was published by abolitionists who, after the Civil War, set about collecting the songs slaves had composed, appearing in *Slave Songs of the United States* (1867) as "The Good Ol' Way," song no. 104. Like so many slave songs, this one became popular among both white and black congregants. Clearly, it suited the purposes of a congregation of striking workers just as well.

5. I Am A Union Woman

words and music: Aunt Molly Jackson

The lyrics, "I was raised in old Kentucky, Kentucky borned and bred, and when I joined the union, they called me a Rooshian Red," concentrate a wealth of information. On the one hand, the facts of Aunt Molly's own life, on the other, the significance of the

Russian Revolution and the threat it posed to the coal operators. Branding organizers "outside agitators" was always (and still is!) a favorite tactic, seeking not only to divide the workers and their supporters but to instill the insidious notion that aspiring to social justice, equality, and freedom were alien to the working class.

The mere fact that the term, "Rooshian Red," could have any impact in Kentucky certainly raises doubts about the region's fabled isolation or the ignorance of its people. Indeed, the convulsive social changes brought about by advancing industrialization (coal mines, railroads, immigrant workers, etc.) had already connected the Appalachians to the rest of the world by the time Jackson composed her song. There had, moreover, been many attempts to organize miners before the National Miners Union (NMU). All had failed, driven out by the treachery and violence of increasingly corporate coal operators. The real outside agitators in this story were the Morgans and Rockefellers who'd been buying up the coalmines in recent years. That the Russian Revolution and communism as an ideal would have an appeal to workers fighting under such conditions is no surprise. The NMU obviously enjoyed the support of at least some miners or "Rooshian Red" would have had no purpose as a term of abuse. Instead, the label was enough to get miners blackballed. Furthermore, the fact that the coal operators used the armed forces of the state as well as their own hired thugs to terrorize striking workers indicates that a significant number of those workers were determined to fight under the NMU's banner. The Harlan County War spanned almost the entire decade of the 1930s. It would have been over very quickly if there hadn't been a large body of miners willing to resist.

6. I Hate The Capitalist System

words: Sarah Ogan Gunning
music: "Sailor On The Deep Blue Sea" by the Carter Family (according to *Hard Hitting Songs for Hard-Hit People*)
additional music: Mat Callahan

This song was first recorded in 1937 by Alan Lomax for the Library of Congress. Gunning was filmed singing it many years later, and that clip was used in the documentary of her life, *Dreadful Memories.*

Barbara Dane also recorded the song in 1973.

One of our most uplifting experiences was performing it at a demonstration on the Bundesplatz in Bern, capital of Switzerland, directly facing the Swiss National

Bank. The demonstration was organized by a truck driver who had seen the terrible conditions in the refugee camps in Greece. She wanted to mobilize support for the safe passage of these people torn from their homes by NATO and U.S.-backed wars. Gunning's song indicted the system responsible.

"Sailor On The Deep Blue Sea" was a song recorded by the Carter Family in 1941, but Gunning wrote her song in the 1930s before the Carter Family's version was released, saying that the music had just come to her mind. There is a resemblance between the melodies of Gunning's and the Carter Family's songs, but this is not unusual, let alone mysterious. Many songs come to be known in a particular version by a particular performer but were in fact taken from an older tune learned earlier. In this case, folklorist Archie Green identified two likely sources, "The Sailor Boy" and "On The Banks Of That Lonely River" either or both of which might have been known to Gunning *and* the Carters.

In any case, without changing the melody in the slightest, I used a totally different harmonization for the guitar accompaniment. I also added a chorus in solidarity with Gunning's stirring words, in part because some controversy persists over whether "capitalist system" was a phrase of her own choosing or was instead the product of "outside" influences.

It has been suggested that being in the orbit of the Communist Party got Gunning to parrot words she would not otherwise have used. This is not credible given abundant evidence to the contrary in Gunning's own lyrics. It is furthermore beyond any doubt that the CP had a mass base in Kentucky and that miners such as Gunning's family knew well what words like "capitalism" and "communism" meant. Apparently it was her choice to rename the song "I Hate the Company Bosses," and there are plenty of reasons she might have done so, the most likely being the prevalence of anticommunism. Anticommunism had dire effects: blacklisting, imprisonment, and death were felt not only by working class people such as Gunning but also by folklorists and academics who may have sought to protect their subjects and themselves from attack. It is to Gunning's great credit that she not only wrote the original text but that she continued singing those words in spite of it all.

7. Mama Don't 'Low No Bush-Wahs Hangin' Around
words and music: Woody Guthrie
additional words and music: Mat Callahan

There are many "Mama Don't 'Low" songs, and Woody's was another variation. The humor in the title and the festive mood created by the music were immediately attractive, as was the fact that this song is not well known. The problem we had was that the lyrics were so particular to the time they were written that they failed to convey the humor Guthrie obviously intended. Modifying the lyrics to, on the one hand, maintain the spirit and, on the other hand, make them funny to present-day audiences was the challenge. Hopefully we succeeded.

As for the music: I chose to "jazz" it up to better convey the party atmosphere Woody invokes when he describes the song's birth at a jam session including Boogie-Woogie piano players, Leadbelly, and himself.

8. Dreadful Memories
words: Sarah Ogan Gunning
music: "Precious Memories" by J.B.F. Wright

This song is obviously a parody, although it doesn't come off as funny, as parodies usually do. It's based on a well-known Christian hymn, "Precious Memories," which is sung at funerals and occasions where nostalgia and reverence for the past are called forth. Gunning was either intentionally or inadvertently mocking such sentiment, using the song's familiarity as a basis to communicate both the desire to escape poverty and the means to achieve that end. We should recall the great migrations that occurred during Gunning's lifetime. Indeed, one was underway in 1938 when Gunning wrote this song. Ultimately millions of workers from the southern states migrated to factories and cities in the North and West. Much of the literature surrounding folk music and artists like Gunning focuses exclusively on place of origin, failing to account for the role of migration. Yet this only underscores Gunning's significance as both a songwriter and emigré. Hers was the fate of a huge number of black and white workers who would flee poverty and degradation in the South, an exodus fraught with hopes of a "promised land" in the North and West. Though the rocks of reality often dashed such hopes, migration had a powerful cultural impact. Historian Michael Denning calls it the *southernization* of American music.

Though she was rediscovered during the folk music revival of the 1960s, appearing at the Newport Folk Festival and others like it, Gunning's songs are still viewed as anomalies or curiosities rather than as representative of an important component of working-class thought. Gunning's address to black and white workers is of particular importance given the racism that, especially in the South, divided and weakened the working class. Gunning's admonition to fight and fight and fight, and her steadfast adherence to the collective "we" obviously set her apart from a generation of "folk singers" who preferred confessional songs, entirely self-absorbed and individualistic. It's my own impression that Gunning embarrassed some folk music devotees because her songs complicated a cherished romantic image. Hers are nonetheless truer to the content and spirit of a great share of the music from which they derived.

9. The Murder Of Harry Simms
words and music: Jim Garland

Harry Simms was not an isolated individual. He was a working-class Jewish kid from Springfield, Massachusetts, who traveled to Birmingham, Alabama, to aid the CPUSA's organizing among sharecroppers. Simms was one of hundreds of young communists who fanned out across the United States joining struggles among agricultural and maritime workers in California, steel workers in Chicago, sharecroppers in Alabama, and miners in Appalachia. This was a social movement as powerful as the more recent civil rights movement, and it explains not only Simms's own willingness to risk life and limb but also the massive response to his murder.

Harry Simms met Jim Garland in Kentucky and the two quickly became fast friends. Garland participated in the memorial held for Simms at the Bronx Coliseum in New York. The moving tribute to Simms, attended by at least twenty thousand (some claim twenty-five thousand), inspired Garland's song.

There are different versions of the song recorded by Pete Seeger, Tao Rodriguez Seeger, and others. The title and text are altered in various ways, for example, the song is often called "The Death of Harry Simms." We chose "murder" instead of "death" because Simms did not die accidentally or through "natural" causes. It was murder, pure and simple. It's also the title of the version that was in *Hard Hitting Songs for Hard-Hit People*. We used the words of this version with one exception: I sing "coal bosses' gun thugs" instead of "dirty capitalist gun thugs" because it's easier to sing at the tempo and in the rhythm of the music.

As for the music, the melody is the original. I altered the harmonization to fit my guitar playing. If I were a banjo player or fiddler, I might have stuck with Pete Seeger's version, but as I needed to keep the rhythm rolling while allowing as many open strings to ring as possible, I used different chords.

10. The Mill Mother's Song (also known as Mill Mother's Lament)
words: Ella May Wiggins
music: "Little Mary Phagan" by John and Rosa Lee Carson (recorded by Vernon Dalhart, Columbia Records, 1925), additional music: Mat Callahan

This is the most famous of Ella May's songs. Its original title was changed from "song" to "lament" in *Hard Hitting Songs*. Reporting on Ella May's murder for the *Labor Defender*, writer Bill Dunne used the title "Mill Mother's Song" and included lyrics not found in other versions. Journalist Margaret Larkin, who befriended Ella May while reporting on the Loray Mills strike, also called it "Mill Mother's Song." We chose to include all the lyrics because all are significant. In fact, the song makes more sense with these added lines.

The music is another example of how the term "folk music" can be misleading. Ella May was no doubt a product of her rural North Carolina background: peasant girl transformed into industrial worker, as so many millions before and since. The music she listened to is reflected in the choices of accompaniment for her lyrics. Most are from popular hits of the day, recorded on shellac and sold to working people to play on Victrolas. The music to this song is a case in point. "Little Mary Phagan" was sung by Vernon Dalhart and was very popular. It's available on YouTube. While Ella May also learned and sang Christian hymns as did virtually all of her peers, she nonetheless chose music for its utility in getting others to join in. In this she was evidently successful. "The bosses hated Ella May," claimed one of her fellow strikers at Loray Mills, "because she made up songs, and was always at the speakings. They aimed to git Ella May."

But this raised further questions for us. When we started work on this song, we were under the impression "Lament" was Ella May's title, we didn't know about the other words or the music she chose to accompany them. We found all this out after performing the song at the James Connolly Festival in Dublin in 2017 (which is also on YouTube). When we learned about the extra words and the original title of the song, we adjusted our interpretation to what we thought were Ella May's original

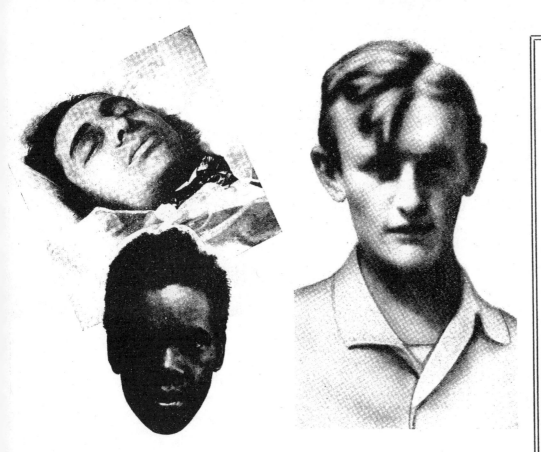

The writer of the first article in this issue, a young worker, Mary Gossman, was on the spot when Ford's gunmen poured lead into the ranks of the starving workers. She described what happened on bloody Monday, the day Ford gave bullets for bread. The destruction of the Ford myth—the great humanitarian—cost the lives of 4 young workers and maimed bodies of 60 more. Foremost in these struggles for the working-class we find the youth. Three of those killed at Dearborn were less than 24 years of age. One of them, Joe York, was a district organizer of the Young Communist League. A month ago it was a Rockefeller thug who killed Harry Simms in Kentucky, another district organizer of the Y.C.L. Three months ago the effects of starvation and bad food took the life of Ronald Edwards, outstanding Negro leader of the Y.C.L. (Their pictures are to the left. York is the large picture.)

These 3 young workers were members of the National Executive Committee of the Y.C.L. All workers—youth and adult, must join the defense movement against this slaughter regime, which shoots down young and old alike.

Workers! Replace Our Fallen Leaders

By MAX WEISS

(Editor of the Young Worker, official organ of the Young Communist League)

More and more it is clear that the capitalist class is using the weapon of bloody terror against the working youth in a desperate effort to prevent them from carrying on the struggle together with the adult workers against hunger, terror and imperialist war.

The terror against the youth has always been sharp but now with the rapid development of the war preparations of the capitalists into actual provocative attacks upon the Soviet Union, the terror against the youth has increased a hundred fold. This increase is due to two main reasons: First, the bosses recognize in the youth one of the most militant sections of the working class army and they therefore try to crush it, secondly, the militancy of the youth places the young workers in the front ranks of the battles of the working class with the result that every attack of the bosses upon the struggles of the working class finds an increasing number of youth victims of boss terror.

A brief glance at the list of young workers killed, jailed or otherwise singled out as objects of capitalist terror is sufficient to convince us of this. Fresh in our minds is the murder of Harry Simms in Kentucky, the murder of York, Leny, and Bussel in Detroit, the jailing of Harry Chandler, youth organizer for the National Miners Union in Pineville, the jailing of Ann Barton and Doris Parks in the same state during the early days of the strike, the six months' jail sentence given Bill Sroka, youth organizer of the National Textile Workers Union, the two and three year sentences passed on Bob Young, Leo Thompson, Stella Rasefski in Pennsylvania for their part in the militant leadership of the Penn-Ohio coal strike of last summer, the criminal syndicalism and sedition charges under which Shantzek and Greenberg, two young workers in Colorado, face twenty year sentences, the attempted legal lynching of the nine Scottsboro Negro boys, the attempted railroading to the electric chair of Jesse Hollins in Oklahoma, the legal lynching of Bonnie Lee Ross in the same state.

The youth must join the fight of the International Labor Defense against boss-terror! Build a strong defense movement!

FREE THE IMPERIAL VALLEY STRIKERS

TWO YEARS ago, on the night of April 1930, a mob of police, deputy-sheriffs, and privately-hired thugs and gangsters, all in the service of the great landowners of the Imperial Valley, burst into a dingy working-class hall in El Centro, California. They were armed with revolvers and sawed-off shotguns.

Sheriff Gillette, notorious gunman of the Imperial Valley bosses, stepped out of the crowd, and ordered all the workers to be chained in groups after which they were marched under heavy guard to the El Centro jail.

Carl Sklar, Los Angeles organizer for the Communist Party; Tetsuji Horiuchi, Japanese organizer of the Trade Union Unity League, were sentenced to serve 3 to 42 years in Folsom Prison. Oscar Erickson, national secretary of the A.W.I.L. Lawrence Emery, of the Marine Workers Industrial Union; Frank Spector, Los Angeles district organizer, I.L.D., and Danny Roxas, Filipino worker secretary of A.W.I.L. in the Imperial Valley, were sentenced to similar terms in San Quentin. Eduardo Herera and Braulio Orosco, Mexican workers, have been deported.

An appeal on the Imperial Valley decisions is being taken to the Supreme Court of the United States. Mass protest freed Spector.

Mass protest by the workers of the country must back up the appeal of the other prisoners, to force the bosses to release them also.

intentions. That is, this is not a lament. It expresses sorrow, to be sure, but it also expresses a fierce determination and that, ultimately, was Ella May's wish.

Listeners who compare will note the additions we made to the melody. This was simply to give the song more musical interest for us. In fact, consulting Dalhart's original tune, we found it maudlin and entirely inappropriate, although that may not have been how it was perceived in 1929. Much popular music of that era was maudlin and pathetic, in the classic sense of pathos or grief. In fact the irony with which today's listeners are so familiar was largely absent from tunes popularized by the music industry at that time.

11. Toiling On Life's Pilgrim Pathway

words: Ella May Wiggins
music: Mat Callahan

The International Labor Defense (ILD) was the legal arm of the International Red Aid network established between 1925 and 1947. The ILD fought many court battles,

Six people wearing shirts emblazoned with "Free Tom Mooney" run onto the track at the final moments of the 1932 Olympics held in Los Angeles.

the most famous of which were the cases of Sacco and Vanzetti, the Scottsboro Boys, Tom Mooney, and Angelo Herndon. The ILD was particularly active in the South and enjoyed widespread support, especially among black workers. The ILD also published the *Labor Defender*, a widely read periodical. Ella May Wiggins was a member of both the National Textile Workers Union and the ILD. Her outspoken advocacy of black and white unity in the South made her a target of both official and vigilante law enforcement.

According to the description given of the music, it was originally a gospel tune. I couldn't get the melody in the book to work, so I wrote something that would fulfill the purpose Ella May obviously intended—get the people singing!

12. Rock-A-Bye Baby
words: unknown
music: traditional .

This song is so well known that it requires little explanation. It's worth noting, however, that it caught Woody Guthrie's attention somehow and he included it in *Hard Hitting Songs*, with the brief introduction: "I heard this song all my life. Mama used to put me to sleep with it. Now here it comes out in Union Form and wakes me up."

13. Going Down The Road Feelin' Bad
words and music: traditional

This song appears twice in *Hard Hitting Songs*. Once with the title "I'm Goin' Down That Road Feeling Bad," once with the title "Blowin' Down This Road," both credited to Woody Guthrie. But Woody didn't write either of them. This points to one of the problems that arose with copyright and the music business. The need to identify an author in order to make money from the sale first of sheet music, later of piano rolls, and later still of sound recordings imposed an artificial constraint on both the natural creative process and on telling the truth. The natural creative process is simply that people use in new ways what they hear and learn from other people; always have, always will. Telling the truth about this cannot be allowed to impede profit-making, however, so we are asked to believe that one author is solely responsible for a song, which in fact is almost never the truth. This song is a case in point. Once recordings started selling, it made its debut as "Lonesome Road Blues" (1924, Henry Ritter). Woody—like all his peers—was told by wise men in the music publishing business that either he would copyright his tune or the money would go to someone else. Indeed, Woody once famously declared (in reference to a different song), "This song is Copyrighted in U.S., under Seal of Copyright #154085, for a period of 28 years, and anybody caught singin' it without our permission, will be mighty good friends of ourn, cause we don't give a dern. Publish it. Write it. Sing it. Swing to it. Yodel it. We wrote it, that's all we wanted to do."

We learned our arrangement from Delaney and Bonnie Bramlett, whose soulful rendition differs markedly from old-time string band arrangements. This only goes to show how widely shared are the feelings expressed in this song. The lyrics we chose from a variety of different versions.

14. Skinnamalinkadoolium
words and music: traditional

This song was among many collected by Alan Lomax on a 1937 visit to Kentucky. It's a retelling of St. Luke's parable of the rich man and Lazarus (Luke 16:19–31). The title and the chorus are nonsense, the purpose of which is playful. Needless to say, this is a time-honored practice in many cultures. Irish and Scottish songs, in particular, abound with this kind of nonsense, and many people in Kentucky were of Irish and Scots-Irish descent. We found the song in *Hard Hitting Songs*, but it wasn't until hearing the recording by Lomax that we really got the spirit of the tune. The song can be heard online at https://lomaxky.omeka.net/items/show/489.

15. A Fool There Was
words and music: Joseph Brandon
additional words: Mat Callahan

Another one from *Hard Hitting Songs*. The music to this song is a variation of "When Johnny Comes Marching Home," which itself is derived from an old English or Scottish ballad. The lyrics required only slight modification to make them relevant today. Indeed, the similarities between Depression-era America and our present situation is clearly evident in this song.

We could find no biographical information on Joseph Brandon but we could find a song of the same title published in 1913: "A Fool There Was." Words by Alexander Dubin. Music by Gustav Benkhart. Published by Shisler Gaskill & Benkhart, Inc., Music Publishers in Philadelphia. It can easily be imagined that Joseph Brandon used the title and wrote original lyrics to the tune, since this was so common a practice.

16. The Preacher And The Slave

words: Joe Hill

music: "The Sweet Bye and Bye" by Joseph P. Webster

This is perhaps Joe Hill's most famous song. The Christian hymn it parodies, "In the Sweet Bye and Bye," has continued in circulation to the present day, having been recorded by singers as diverse as Elvis Presley and Louis Armstrong. Apparently Harry McClintock of "Big Rock Candy Mountain" fame was the first to perform Hill's parody. According to the writer Wallace Stegner, "McClintock . . . sang Joe Hill's 'Pie in the Sky' song on Burnside Street in Portland, reading it off an envelope or laundry tag Joe Hill had handed him. That was the first time 'Pie in the Sky' was sung on the street. At other times McClintock sang some other ones of Joe Hill, including 'The Wobbly Casey Jones.'"[1] But this is only part of the story.

As reported on the Bluegrass Messenger website: "To counteract management sending in the Salvation Army band to cover up the Wobbly speakers, Joe Hill wrote parodies of Christian hymns so that union members could sing along with the Salvation Army band, but with their own purposes. Hill's most famous parody was of 'In The Sweet Bye And Bye,' which became 'There'll Be Pie In The Sky When You Die (That's A Lie).' 'Then,' according to Lomax, 'they convulsed their hard boiled audience with irreverent parodies of Salvation Army tear-jerkers' many of them Joe Hill compositions.'"[2]

To bring the story full circle, it was Harry McClintock's version of "Big Rock Candy Mountain" that appeared in the Coen brothers film *O Brother, Where Art Thou?*. The film, in turn, had the effect of enchanting a new generation of music lovers, inspiring a "folk music revival" at the beginning of the twenty-first century.

1   *Conversations with Wallace Stegner on Western History and Literature* (Salt Lake City: University of Utah Press, 1990), 70.

2   http://www.bluegrassmessengers.com/harry-%E2%80%9Chaywire-mac%E2%80%9D-mcclintock--1928-.aspx.

The renewed interest in McClintock (who died in San Francisco in 1957) led some curious listeners to Joe Hill, the Wobblies, and the *Little Red Songbook*. The latter, first published in 1909 and renewed periodically ever since, stands as a living refutation of virtually every pious claim made about workers, music, authenticity, and class consciousness. I have no idea if the Coen brothers had this in mind, but the irreverence of the "Soggy Bottom Boys" certainly jibes with Joe Hill's parodic style, considering that Foggy Bottom is a nickname for the U.S. State Department.

17. Joe Hill

words: Alfred Hayes
music: Earl Robinson

When Yvonne heard Paul Robeson sing this song, she was immediately inspired to include it here, even though it is not in *Hard Hitting Songs*. Robeson's rendering is legendary, as were his many appearances on behalf of workers and oppressed people the world over. Robeson, who jeopardized a highly successful career to side with the workers, defiantly stated: "The artist must take sides. He must elect to fight for freedom or slavery. I have made my choice. I had no alternative." When his passport was revoked by the U.S. government in 1957, Robeson sang over the telephone to sold-out gatherings in London and Wales. His artistry and his example continue to pose a challenge to those who bid us succumb to the lures of fame and fortune just as they provide inspiration to those who choose to fight for humanity's emancipation.

It is worthy of note that Joan Baez performed "Joe Hill" at the Woodstock Festival in 1969, a performance preserved in the film of that festival. While Baez's choice was somewhat enigmatic given that most of the audience had no recollection of the song or who Joe Hill was, it was nonetheless a fitting tribute and a reminder of what is enduring in a culture of consumption and disposability.

18. We Have Fed You All For A Thousand Years

words: An Unknown Proletarian
music: Mat Callahan

I found this poem in the *Little Red Songbook* back in the 1970s. I remember sitting backstage at some rally or other and strumming some chords. These later solidified into an appropriate musical accompaniment for this profound and moving text. Though I recorded this back then with Sandy Callahan, my partner at the time, we decided to include a new recording here for ready accessibility.

19. No More Mournin'

words: John Handcox
music: "Oh, Freedom" (author unknown)

This song is clearly derived from "Oh Freedom," a song first recorded in 1931 and subsequently popularized by Odetta and Joan Baez (who sang it at the March on Washington in 1963). Handcox often used this approach, making slight but significant modifications to well-known songs for the purpose of building unity in the struggle. Handcox joined the Southern Tenant Farmers Union in 1935 and in 1937 was recorded by Charles Seeger and Sidney Robertson for the Library of Congress. The STFU organized black and white sharecroppers and not surprisingly was viciously attacked by the big landowners. Handcox was in the thick of things as a farmer and organizer. Indeed, it was as an organizer that Handcox was primarily occupied, his prodigious songwriting done in service to that cause. Unlike many of the other songwriters in this collection, Handcox continued into the 1980s, writing songs critical of Ronald Reagan, for example. He died in 1992.

Pete Seeger writes in an afterword to the recent edition of *Hard Hitting Songs for Hard-Hit People* that the only change made to the original was the photo of John Handcox discovered years after the original book was published. Seeger further notes that Handcox's whereabouts were unknown at the time of the book's publication, and only later was Handcox located and found to still be active in labor struggles and songwriting.

20. Commonwealth Of Toil

words: Ralph Chaplin

music: "Nelly Gray" by Benjamin Hanby[3]

First published in 1917 in a book of rebel verses entitled *When the Leaves Come Out*, this song is a both a timeless testament and a monument to a pivotal moment in world history. It cannot be a coincidence that the Russian Revolution took place the same year. Nor is it likely that Chaplin was unaware of the Easter Rising of 1916 given the close relationship of James Connolly, a leader of the Rising, with the IWW of which Chaplin and Connolly were members. Chaplin, who is best remembered for composing "Solidarity Forever" to the tune of another great abolitionist song, "John Brown's Body," was obviously fond of using popular melodies that already had revolutionary associations.

We added our own harmonization to enhance the anthemic quality of this stirring, visionary text.

---

3   Hanby was an abolitionist. He composed "Nelly Gray" in 1856. It soon became widely popular and is performed to this day.

WORDS
AND
MUSIC

Come All You Coal Miners

words and music: Sarah Ogan Gunning

1.

Come all you coal miners wherever you may be
And listen to a story that I'll relate to thee
My name is nothing extry, but the truth to you I'll tell
I am a coal miner's wife, I'm sure l wish you well.

2.

Coal mining is the most dangerousest work in our land today
With plenty of dirty slavin' work, and very little pay.
Coal miner, won't you wake up, and open your eyes and see
What the dirty capitalist system is doing to you and me.

3.

They take your very life blood, they take our children's lives
Take fathers away from children, and husbands away from wives.
Coal miners, won't you organize wherever you may be
And make this a land of freedom for workers like you and me.

4.

Dear miners, they will slave you 'til you can't work no more
And what will you get for your living but a dollar in a company store
A tumble-down shack to live in, snow & rain pours in the top
You have to pay the company rent, your paying never stops.

5.

I am a coal miner's wife, I'm sure l wish you well.
Let's sink this capitalist system in the darkest pits of hell.

There Is Mean Things Happening In This Land

words: John Handcox/additional words Mat Callahan
music: traditional arranged by Mat Callahan and Yvonne Moore

1.
There is mean things happening in this land
There is mean things happening in this land,
Oh the rich man boasts and brags
While the poor man goes in rags
There is mean things happening in this land

4.
There is mean things happening in this land
There is mean things happening in this land,
Lots of groceries on the shelves,
But we have none for ourselves
There is mean things happening in this land

2.
There is mean things happening in this land
There is mean things happening in this land,
Oh, the farmer cannot eat,
'Cause he's raised too much wheat,
There is mean things happening in this land

5.
There is mean things happening in this land
There is mean things happening in this land,
But when workers all refuse
To be blinded and abused,
There'll be GOOD things happening in this land

3.
There is mean things happening in this land
There is mean things happening in this land,
Too much cotton in our sacks
So we have none on our backs
There is mean things happening in this land

6.
There'll be GOOD things happening in this land
There'll be GOOD things happening in this land
When the workers take a stand
And unite in a solid band,
There'll be GOOD things happening in this land

I Am A Girl Of Constant Sorrow

words: Sarah Ogan Gunning
music: traditional

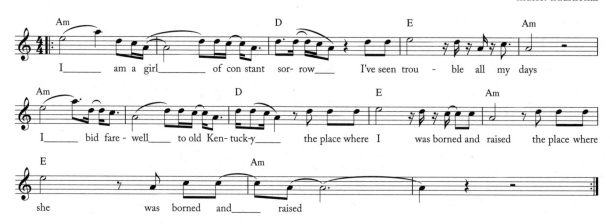

1.
I am a girl of constant sorrow
I've seen trouble all my days
I bid farewell to old Kentucky
The place where I was borned and raised

2.
My mother, how I hated to leave her
Mother dear, who now is dead
But I had to go and leave her
So my children could have bread

3.
Well, our clothes are always ragged,
And our feet are always bare
And I know if there is a heaven
That we all are going there

4.
Goodbye my friends I hate to leave you
It grieves me so that we must part
For I know we all are hungry
Oh, it almost breaks my heart

5.
Well, we call this Hell on earth friends
I must tell you all goodbye
Oh, I know you all are hungry
Oh my darling friends, don't cry

Come On Friends And Let's Go Down

words: Sarah Ogan Gunning
music: "The Good Ol' Way" (unknown author)

1.
As I went down on the picket line
To keep them scabs out of the mine
Who's a going to win the strike
Come on and we'll show you the way

CHORUS

2.
Went out one morning before daylight
And I was sure we'd have a fight
But the capitalist scurvy'd run away
And we went back the very next day

CHORUS

3.
We all went out on the railroad track
To meet them scabs and turn them back
We win that strike I'm glad to say
Come on, and we'll show you the way

CHORUS

I Am A Union Woman

words and music: Aunt Molly Jackson

1. I am a Un-ion wom-an, as brave as I__ can be I do not like the bos-ses and the bos - ses don't like me

Join the N. M. U. come and join the N. M. U. join the N. M. U. come and join the N. M. U.

1.
I am a Union woman,
As brave as I can be
I do not like the bosses
and the bosses don't like me

CHORUS

2.
I was raised in old Kentucky,
Kentucky borned and bred
And when I joined the union,
Well they called me a Rooshian Red

CHORUS

3.
My husband asked the boss for a job
This is the words he said:
"Bill Jackson, I can't work you, sir, 'cause
Your wife's a Rooshian Red"

CHORUS

4.
These is the worst times
That I have ever saw
You get shot down by gun-thugs
You get framed up by the law

CHORUS

5.
Our bosses ride fine horses
And we walk in the mud
Their banner is the dollar sign
And ours is striped with blood

CHORUS

6.
If you want to get your freedom
Also your liberty
Join the dear old N.M.U.
And come along with me

CHORUS

I Hate The Capitalist System

words: Sarah Ogan Gunning
music: "Sailor on the Deep Blue Sea"/additional music: Mat Callahan

Mama Don't 'Low No Bush-Wahs Hangin' Around

words and music: Woody Guthrie
additional words and music: Mat Callahan

1.

Come here Mama, take a look at Kate
Comin' down the road in a Cadillac 8
Mama don't 'low no bush-wahs hangin' 'round
Hardly recognize her in that rig
Feather boa and a curly wig
Mama don't 'low no bush-wahs hangin' 'round

CHORUS

2.

Big fat man with a pocket full of money
Took my likker and he took my honey
Mama don't 'low no bush-wahs hangin' 'round
Banker come to take my farm
He took my gal off under his arm
Mama don't 'low no bush-wahs hangin' 'round

CHORUS

3.

Rich man swagger big and proud
Thinks he's smart but he's just loud
Mama don't 'low no bush-wahs hangin' 'round
Thinks we're laughing at his jokes
When we're just seeing through the hoax
Mama don't 'low no bush-wahs hangin' 'round

CHORUS

4.

I'm just an old hard working man
I ride 'em like I find 'em do the best I can
Mama don't 'low no bush-wahs hangin' 'round
Take my stand at the Union Hall
An injury to one is an injury to all
Mama don't 'low no bush-wahs hangin' 'round

CHORUS

Dreadful Memories

words: Sarah Ogan Gunning
music: "Precious Memories" by J.B.F. Wright

1.
Dreadful memories, how they linger,
How they ever flood my soul.
How the workers and their children
Die from hunger and from cold.

2.
Hungry fathers, wearied mothers,
Living in those dreadful shacks,
Little children cold and hungry
With no clothing on their backs.

3.
Dreadful gun thugs and stool pigeons
Always flock around our door.
What's the crime that we've committed?
Nothing, only that we're poor.

4.
When I think of all the heartaches
And all the things that we have been through,
Then I wonder how much longer
And what a working man can do.

5.
We will have to join the union,
They will help you find a way
How to get a better living
And for your work get better pay.

6.
Really, friends, it doesn't matter
Whether you are black or white.
The only way you'll ever change things
Is to fight and fight and fight.

The Murder Of Harry Simms

words and music: Jim Garland

1.

Comrades, listen to my story, comrades, listen to my song
I will tell you of a hero, who now is dead and gone
I will tell you of a young boy, whose age was just nineteen
He was the bravest union man, that I have ever seen

2.

Harry Simms was a pal of mine, we labored side by side
Expecting to be shot on sight, or taken for a ride
By the coal bosses' gun thugs, that roam from town to town
To shoot and kill our Comrades, where'er they may be found

3.

Harry Simms and I were parted at five o'clock that day
Be careful, My dear Comrade, to Harry I did say.
I must do my duty, was his reply to me,
If I get killed by gun thugs, don't grieve after me.

4.

Harry Simms was walking up the track, this bright sunshiny day
He was a youth of courage, his step was light and gay
We did not know the gun thugs was hiding on the way
To kill our dear young comrade this bright sunshiny day

5.

Harry Simms was killed on Brush Creek, in nineteen thirty-two
He organized the Y.C.L., also the N.M.U.
He gave his life in struggle, that was all that he could do
He died to save the union, also for me and you

6.

Comrades we must vow today, this is one thing we must do.
Must organize the miners in the dear old N.M.U.
And get a million volunteers into the Y.C.L.
And sink this rotten system in the deepest pits of Hell.

The Mill Mother's Song

words: Ella May Wiggins
music: "Little Mary Phagan" by J. and R. Carson/additional music: Mat Callahan

1.

We leave our homes in the morning, we kiss our children good bye,
While we slave for the bosses, our children scream and cry.
And when we draw our money, our grocery bills to pay,
Not a cent to spend for clothing, not a cent to lay away.
And on that very evening our little son will say:
"I need some shoes, mother, and so does sister May."

2.

How it grieves the heart of a mother you everyone must know.
But we can't buy for our children, our wages are too low.
It is for our little children, that seems to us so dear,
But for us nor them, dear workers, the bosses do not care.
But understand, all workers, our union they do fear.
Let's stand together, workers and have a union here.

3.

Now listen to me, workers, both women and men
We are sure to win our union, if all would enter in.
I hope this will be a warning, I hope you will understand,
And help us win our victory and lend to us a hand.

Toiling On Life's Pilgrim Pathway

words: Ella May Wiggins
music: Mat Callahan

1.
Toiling on life's pilgrim pathway
Wheresoever you may be,
It will help you fellow workers
If you will join the I.L.D.

CHORUS

2.
When the bosses cut your wages
And you toil the labor free
Come and join the textile union
Also join the I.L.D.

CHORUS

3.
Now our leaders are in prison
But I hope they will soon be free
Come and join the textile union
Also join the I.L.D.

CHORUS

4.
Now the South is hedged in darkness
Although they begin to see
Come and join the textile union
Also join the I.L.D.

CHORUS

Rock-A-Bye Baby

words: unknown
music: traditional

1.
Rock-a-bye Baby on the tree top
When you grow up you'll work in a shop
When you are married your wife will work, too
So that the rich will have nothing to do.

2.
Hush-a-bye Baby on the tree top
When you grow old your wages will stop
When you have spent the little you've made
First to the poor house then to the grave

Going Down The Road Feelin' Bad

words and music: traditional

Verse 1

1. Go-in' down the road feel-ing bad__ go-in' down the road____ feel-ing bad__

go-in' down the road____ feel-ing bad,__ oh, Lord ain't gon-na be treat-ed this way__

Verse 2

2. Ma-ma said, son, don't go way down there_ she told me,____ don't go way down there,_ she said,

son, don't go way down there,__ oh, Lord don't want to be treat-ed this way__ 3. Some-bo-dy

Verse 3

help me__ get on a-way from here won't you help me get on a way from here_ some-bo-dy

help me__ get on a-way from here_ oh Lord, Lord__ ain't gon-na be treat-ed this way__ 4. Well I'm

Verse 4

go-ing where the wa-ter tastes like wine yes I'm__ go-ing where the wa-ter__ tastes like wine well I'm

go-ing where the wa-ter__ tastes like wine oh Lord, Lord__ don't wan-na be treat-ed this way__ 5. Well

Verse 5

go-in' down the road feel-ing bad__ go in' down the road____ feel-ing bad__

go-in' down the road____ feel-ing bad, oh, Lord ain't gon-na be treat-ed this way__

Skinnamalinkadoolium

words and music: traditional

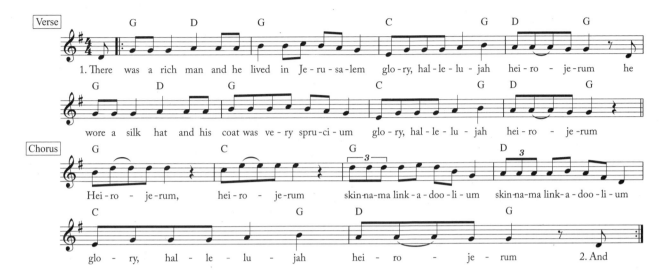

1.
There was a rich man and he lived in Jerusalem,
Glory, hallelujah hei-ro-je-rum
He wore a silk hat and his coat was very sprucium
Glory, hallelujah hei-ro-je-rum

CHORUS

2.
And at his gate there sat a human wreckium
Glory hallelujah hei-ro-je-rum
He wore a bowler hat & the rim was round his neckium
Glory hallelujah hei-ro-je-rum

CHORUS

3.
That poor man asked for a piece of bread and cheesium
Glory hallelujah hei-ro-je-rum
The rich man answered, "I'll call for a policeium"
Glory hallelujah hei-ro-je-rum

CHORUS

4.
The poor man died and his soul went to heavium
Glory hallelujah hei-ro-je-rum
And he danced with the saints til quarter past ellevium
Glory hallelujah hei-ro-je-rum

CHORUS

5.
And there he dwelt in Abraham's bosium
Glory hallelujah hei-ro-je-rum
Fraternizing there with scores of other Jewseum
Glory hallelujah hei-ro-je-rum

CHORUS

6.
The rich man died but he didn't fare so welleum
Glory hallelujah hei-ro-je-rum
He couldn't go to heaven so he had to go to helleum
Glory hallelujah hei-ro-je-rum

CHORUS

7.
The rich man asked for to have a consolium
Glory hallelujah hei-ro-je-rum
The devil only answered, "Just shovel on the coalium!"
Glory hallelujah hei-ro-je-rum

CHORUS

8.
The moral of this story is that riches are no jokium
Glory hallelujah hei-ro-je-rum
We'll all go to heaven because we are stony brokium
Glory hallelujah hei-ro-je-rum

CHORUS

A Fool There Was

words and music: Joseph Brandon
additional words Mat Callahan

1.
A fool there was and he had no job,
Even as you and I
And he didn't want to steal or rob,
Even as you and I
And so each day he thinner grew,
He tightened his belt a notch or two,
'Til it nearly cut him right in two,
Even as you and I

2.
He voted for what he thought was change,
Even as you and I
When nothing did he thought it strange,
Even as you and I
But though the promises lost their shine
He couldn't help thinking it oh so kind
They'd saved him a place in the old soup line
Even as you and I

3.
He watched depression growing worse
Even as you and I
As bankers looted the public purse
Even as you and I
They told him this was a country grand
With plenty of everything in the land
So he starved to death with a flag in his hand
Even as you and I

The Preacher And The Slave

words: Joe Hill
music: "The Sweet Bye and Bye" by Joseph P. Webster

1.
Long-haired preachers come out every night,
Try to tell you what's wrong and what's right;
But when asked how 'bout something to eat
They will answer with voices so sweet:

CHORUS

2.
And the starvation army they play,
And they sing and they clap and they pray.
Till they get all your coin on the drum,
Then they tell you when you are on the bum:

CHORUS

3.
If you fight hard for children and wife
Try to get something good in this life
You're a sinner and bad man, they tell,
When you die you will sure go to hell.

CHORUS

4.
Workingmen of all countries unite,
Side by side we for freedom will fight;
When the world and its wealth we have gained
To the grafters we'll sing this refrain:

CHORUS

Joe Hill

words: Alfred Hayes
music: Earl Robinson

1.
I dreamed I saw Joe Hill last night,
Alive as you and me.
Says I "But Joe, you're ten years dead"
"I never died" says he,
"I never died" says he.

2.
"In Salt Lake City, Joe" says I,
Him standing by my bed
"They framed you on a murder charge"
Says Joe "but I ain't dead"
Says Joe "but I ain't dead"

3.
"The Copper Bosses killed you Joe,
They shot you Joe" says I.
"Takes more than guns to kill a man"
Says Joe "I didn't die"
Says Joe "I didn't die"

4.
And standing there as big as life
And smiling with his eyes.
Says Joe "What they can never kill
Went on to organize,
Went on to organize"

5.
From San Diego up to Maine,
In every mine and mill,
Where workers fight and organize,
It's there you find Joe Hill,
It's there you find Joe Hill!

6.
I dreamed I saw Joe Hill last night,
Alive as you and me.
Says I "But Joe, you're ten years dead"
"I never died" said he,
"I never died" said he.

We Have Fed You All For A Thousand Years

words: An Unknown Proletarian

music: Mat Callahan

1. We have fed you all___ for a thou-sand years   and here we are still un-fed_

but there's nev-er a dol-lar of all your wealth_   that doesn't mark the work-ers dead_

we have giv-en our best___ to give you rest__   and you lie_ on crim-son wool

but if blood be the price of all your wealth_   then good God we have paid in___ full_

2. There is nev-er a mind_ blown sky-ward now_____   but we're bur-ied a-live_ for___ you_____

___ there is nev-er a wreck_ drifts shore-ward_ now_____   but we are it's ghast - ly crew_____

___ go reck-on our _ dead by_ the forg-es red_____   and the fac-to-ries where we___ spin_____

___ Lord, if blood be the price of your curs-ed
wealth_____ good God we have paid it____
in_____

But we are its ghastly crew
Go reckon our dead by the forges red
And the factories where we spin
Lord, if blood be the price of your cursed wealth
Good God we have paid it in

1.
We have fed you all for a thousand years
And here we are still unfed
But there's never a dollar of all your wealth
That's doesn't mark the workers dead
We have given our best to give you rest
And you lie on crimson wool
But if blood be the price of all your wealth
Then good God we have paid in full

3.
We have fed you all for a thousand years
For that was our doom, you know
From the days when you chained us in your fields
To the strike a week ago
You have taken our lives, and our babies and wives
And we're told it's your legal share
But if blood be the price of your lawful wealth
Then good God we have bought it fair

2.
There is never a mine blown skyward now
But we're buried alive for you
There is never a wreck drifts shoreward now

No More Mournin'

words: John Handcox
music: "Oh, Freedom" (author unknown)

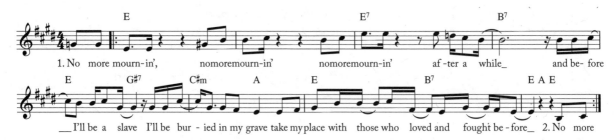

1. No more mourn-in', nomoremourn-in' nomoremourn-in' af-ter a while_ and be- fore ___ I'll be a slave I'll be bur - ied in my grave take my place with those who loved and fought be - fore_ 2. No more

1.
No more mournin', no more mournin'
No more mournin' after a while
And before I'll be a slave
I'll be buried in my grave
Take my place with those who
Loved and fought before

2.
No more cryin', no more cryin'
No more cryin' after a while

3.
No more weepin', no more weepin'
No more weepin' after a while

4.
No more sorrows, no more sorrows
No more sorrows after a while

5.
Oh, freedom, oh, freedom
Oh, freedom after a while

6.
No more slavery, no more slavery
No more slavery after a while
And before I'll be a slave
I'll be buried in my grave
Take my place with those who
Loved and fought before

The Commonwealth Of Toil

words: Ralph Chaplin
music: "Nelly Gray" by Benjamin Hanby

1.

In the gloom of mighty cities mid the roar of whirling wheels,
We are toiling on like chattel slaves of old,
And our masters hope to keep us ever thus beneath their heels,
And to coin our very life blood into gold.

CHORUS

2.

They would keep us cowed and beaten cringing meekly at their feet.
They would stand between each worker and his bread.
Shall we yield our lives up to them for the bitter crusts we eat?
Shall we only hope for heaven when we're dead?

CHORUS

3.

They have laid our lives out for us to the utter end of time.
Shall we stagger on beneath their heavy load?
Shall we let them live forever in their gilded halls of crime,
With our children doomed to toil beneath their goad?

CHORUS

4.

When our cause is all triumphant and we claim our Mother Earth,
And the nightmare of the present fades away,
We shall live with love and laughter we who now are little worth,
And we'll not regret the price we have to pay.

CHORUS

ON TO CLEVELAND

OCTOBER 8th—9th, 1932

To the 5th National Convention of the
International Labor Defense

PREPARE for WORLD CONGRESS in NOVEMBER

SOURCES

FIRST AND FOREMOST, *HARD HITTING SONGS FOR HARD-HIT PEOPLE* IS BOTH THE source of most of the songs in this collection but also important biographical information about the songwriters. For example, in the biographical sketches, we used a statement John Handcox made that we found in *Hard Hitting Songs*. We later discovered that this statement was recorded in 1937 when Handcox recorded many of his songs for the Library of Congress. This recording session can be accessed online at https://www.loc.gov/item/afc9999005.6544.

A great deal more information is both necessary and available from other sources listed below. These can be divided into four kinds: primary sources,[1] songbooks, histories of music and politics, and biographies or studies of particular individuals. For example, Ella May Wiggins's story is told in the *Labor Defender* article we've reproduced in this book. She is also referred to in songbooks and histories of American folk music and has a biography written about her. There are also a handful of classic texts which virtually every folklorist or historian refers to. These texts include album liner notes and songbooks as well as histories and are listed here to aid the curious. For ease of use, we will provide general sources first, then under each individual's name we will list sources specific to that person.

Primary sources such as the *Labor Defender* were consulted and examples copied for the reader's benefit. These are obtainable at https://www.marxists.org/history/usa/pubs/labordefender/index.htm and at the History Is a Weapon website: http://www.historyisaweapon.com/indextrue.html.

---

1   Primary sources include, for example, state or church records of birth, marriage, and death; testimony given in court or in recorded interviews; and artifacts such as the *Labor Defender*.

Additional primary sources may be harder to get, requiring academic credentials. When such credentials can be obtained, Tamiment Library (https://library.nyu.edu/locations/the-tamiment-library-robert-f-wagner-labor-archives/) and the Schomburg Library (https://www.nypl.org/about/locations/schomburg) have many relevant documents.

Cohen, Ronald, and Dave Samuelson. *Songs for Political Action*. 10-CD set with book. Hambergen: Bear Family Records, 1996. https://www.bear-family.com/various-history-songs-for-political-action-10-cd.html.

Denisoff, R. Serge. *Great Day Coming: Folk Music and the American Left*. Urbana: University of Illinois Press, 1971.

Denning, Michael. *The Cultural Front: The Laboring of American Culture in the Twentieth Century*. New York: Verso, 1997.

Filene, Benjamin. *Romancing the Folk: Public Memory and American Roots Music*. Chapel Hill: University of North Carolina Press, 2000.

Foner, Philip S. *American Labor Songs of the Nineteenth Century*. Urbana: University of Illinois Press, 1975.

Fowke, Edith, and Joe Glazer. *Songs of Work and Freedom*. Chicago: Roosevelt University, 1960.

Greenway, John. *American Folksongs of Protest*. Philadelphia: University of Pennsylvania Press, 1953.

Lieberman, Robbie, *My Song Is My Weapon: People's Songs, American Communism, and the Politics of Culture, 1930–50*. Urbana: University of Illinois Press, 1989.

Lomax, Alan. *The Folk Songs of North America*. New York: Doubleday Books, 1960.

Lynch, Timothy P., *Strike Songs of the Depression*. Jackson: University Press of Mississippi, 2001.

Reuss, Richard A., and JoAnne C. Reuss. *American Folk Music and Left-Wing Politics, 1927–1957*. Lanham, MD: Scarecrow Press, 2000.

Smith, Harry. *Anthology of American Folk Music*. 6 LPs with program notes. New York: Folkways Records, 1952.

Ella May Wiggins

Ella May Wiggins Memorial Committee, https://ellamaywiggins.com/.

Horton, Kristina. *Martyr of Loray Mill: Ella May and the 1929 Textile Workers' Strike in Gastonia, North Carolina.* Jefferson, NC: McFarland, 2015.

Huber, Patrick, "Ella May Wiggins and *The Mill Mother's Song.*" Old Hat Records, http://oldhatrecords.com/ResearchGGEMWiggins.html.

Hunt, Max, "Working-Class Hero: A Q&A with Kristina Horton on the Martyr of Loray Mill," Mountain Xpress, January 15, 2017, https://mountainx.com/arts/working-class-hero-a-qa-with-author-kristina-horton-on-the-martyr-of-loray-mill/.

Aunt Molly Jackson, Jim Garland, and Sarah Ogan Gunning

Sources of information about Aunt Molly Jackson, Sarah Ogan Gunning, and Jim Garland range from tape-recorded interviews made in the 1960s by Archie Green and Ellen Stekert, to Mary Elizabeth Barnicle's extensive interviews and field notes, to recollections of people who knew them including those of Pete Seeger, Woody Guthrie, and Alan Lomax. Many of these have been compiled by Shelly Romalis in her book *Pistol Packin' Mama: Aunt Molly Jackson and the Politics of Folksong.* There is also the documentary film of Sarah Ogan Gunning's life by Mimi Pickering, *Dreadful Memories* (1988), which includes late performances by Gunning along with reminiscences by relatives, neighbors and others who knew her. Another key source is Jim Garland's autobiography.

Last but not least is Sarah Ogan Gunning's own album, *Girl of Constant Sorrow*, released by Folk-Legacy Records. Included with the CD are Archie Green's concise biography of Gunning and informative song notes (see link below).

Cohen, Ronald, and Dave Samuelson. *Songs for Political Action.* 10-CD set with book. Hambergen: Bear Family Records, 1996. https://www.bear-family.com/various-history-songs-for-political-action-10-cd.html.

Garland, Jim. *Welcome the Traveler Home: Jim Garland's Story of the Kentucky Mountains.* Edited by Julie S. Audery. Lexington: University Press of Kentucky, 1983.

Gunning, Sarah Ogan. *Girl of Constant Sorrow*. Compact disc. Folk-Legacy
    Records: http://www.folk-legacy.com/store/scripts/prodView.asp?idproduct=54.
Pickering, Mimi, dir. *Dreadful Memories: The Life of Sara Ogan Gunning*. Film.
    Whitesburg, KY: Appalshop Films, 1988. http://www.folkstreams.net/film-
    detail.php?id=164.
Romalis, Shelley: *Pistol Packin' Mama: Aunt Molly Jackson and the Politics of Folksong*.
    University of Illinois Press, 1999.
"The Songs of Sarah Ogan Gunning." Folk Archive. http://www.folkarchive.de/
    gunning.html.

John Handcox

Core, Richard. "Union Organizer, Songwriter John L. Handcox Is Dead at 88,"
    L.A. Times, September 25, 1992, http://articles.latimes.com/1992-09-25/local/
    me-1029_1_union-organizer.
Handcox, John L. *Songs, Poems, and Stories of the Southern Tenant Farmers*. Compact
    disc, 978-0-937058-90-9. Compiled by Mark Allen Jackson. Morgantown:
    West Virginia University Press, c. 2004.
Honey, Michael K. "John Handcox," Black Past, March 24, 2015, https://www.
    blackpast.org/african-american-history/handcox-john-l-1904-1992.
Honey, Michael K. *Sharecropper's Troubadour: John L. Handcox, the Southern Tenant
    Farmers' Union, and the African American Song Tradition*. Palgrave Studies in
    Oral History. New York: Palgrave Macmillan, 2013.

Paul Robeson

Duberman, Martin. *Paul Robeson*. New York: The New Press, 1995.
"The Many Faces of Paul Robeson," National Archives, August 15, 2016. https://
    www.archives.gov/education/lessons/robeson.
"Paul Robeson Archive," Marxists Internet Archive. https://www.marxists.org/
    archive/robeson/.
Robeson, Paul. *Here I Stand*. New York: Othello Associates, 1958.
Robeson, Paul. *Paul Robeson Speaks*. Secaucus, NJ: Citadel, 2002.

White, Claytee Dee. "Paul Robeson (1898–1976)," Black Past. http://www.blackpast.org/aah/robeson-paul-1898-1976.

Wright, Charles H. *Robeson: Labor's Forgotten Champion*. Detroit: Balamp Publishing, 1975.

Joe Hill

Chaplin, Ralph. "Joe Hill: A Biography," November 1923 issue of the *Industrial Pioneer*, Chicago: General Executive Board, Industrial Workers of the World: 23–26. Vern Smith Papers #5172. Kheel Center for Labor-Management Documentation and Archives, Cornell University Library. http://rmc.library.cornell.edu/EAD/htmldocs/KCL05172.html.

Rosemont, Franklin. *Joe Hill: The IWW & the Making of a Revolutionary Workingclass Counterculture*. Oakland: PM Press, 2015.

Ralph Chaplin

Chaplin, Ralph. *Bars and Shadows: The Prison Poems of Ralph Chaplin*. London: George Allen, 1922. https://archive.org/details/barsshadows00chaprich.

Chaplin, Ralph. *The Centralia Conspiracy*. Chicago: IWW Publishing Bureau, 1920. https://www.gutenberg.org/files/10725/10725-h/10725-h.htm.

Chaplin, Ralph. *When the Leaves Come Out*. 1917. https://en.wikisource.org/wiki/When_the_Leaves_Come_Out.

Chaplin, Ralph. "Why I Wrote Solidarity Forever." *American West* 5, no. 1 (January 1968). https://www.iww.org/history/icons/solidarity_forever/1.

Chaplin, Ralph. *Wobbly, the Rough and Tumble Story of an American Radical*. Chicago: University of Chicago Press, 1948.

Appendix

Music and Historical Memory

(speech delivered to a general assembly at Berklee College of Music, 2010)

Music can remember what History forgets. Attesting to this fact is a great body of music commemorating people and events often ignored or obscured by prevailing historical accounts. This is not confined to ballads or folk songs of the past but is the subject of contemporary compositions as well.

MUSIC AND MEMORY HAVE ALWAYS BEEN INSEPARABLE. AFTER ALL, MEMORY IS THE name of the goddess who was Mother of the Muses. The Muses, according to the poet Hesiod, "were nine like-minded daughters, whose one thought is singing, and whose hearts are free from care . . . who delight with song . . . telling of things that are, that will be, and that were with voices joined in harmony." They called on Hesiod to sing their praises, but they did so with a challenge: "You rustic shepherd, shame: bellies you are, not men! We know enough to make up lies which are convincing, but we also have the skill, when we've a mind, to speak the truth."[1]

That the nine muses were the daughters of Memory and not another Goddess is explained by the fact that their number corresponds to the gestation period of human beings. Memory lay with Zeus nine nights to produce nine daughters and in the marvelous mathematics of myth our story begins with the renewal of human life upon this earth. Memory serves unfolding and rebirth, not the mere storage of information.

This interpretation is supported further by the fact that Memory was the protectress of Eleuther's Hills—"Eleuther" meaning "freedom" in Greek. What greater gift could there be than to rejuvenate our bodies while freeing our imaginations? Therefore, the Greeks of Hesiod's time thought memory should be studied, practiced, and improved in an ordering process that would enable the orator, the poet, the actor, or musician to deliver public performance without recourse to writing. Indeed, writing was viewed as a pale substitute for memory, merely reminding when

---

1   Hesiod, *Theogony*, translated by Dorothea Wender (London: Penguin Books, 1973).

one needed to remember. Writing is an external sign whereas memory comes from within. Therefore, writing is less reliable as a source for what it is most important to know. Written words cannot themselves convey the method by which memory must be practiced and made a guarantor of learning. Regardless of what we think of writing now—and in the intervening centuries the phrase "it is written" was used to lend legitimacy to any claim—there is something to be said for this approach, as musicians and actors certainly know. We will return to this point later on. For now, it's enough to recall that memory is a crucial component of learning. But just as there are different things to learn, there are different kinds of memory. And music plays a role in all of them.

The first kind of memory is what I call immediate or instant recall for present use. This requires the honing of skills by repetition in order to perform specific tasks. It's not surprising that music would serve as a mnemonic or memory aid since rhythm and melody are delightful, they unite the body and mind, and children in particular quickly and easily respond to them. To help memorize the alphabet, times tables, and other recipes or formulas, simple songs have been devised. Not only does music alleviate the drudgery of repetition and drill but it brings immediately to life the stored information when it has not been used for some time. In fact, scales or rhythms are themselves assemblages of notes and beats by which we remember what to play. It is of course useful that music can be written down and that sight reading is a necessary skill in many situations. But this can only be a supplement or aid for what is ultimately an auditory phenomenon, not a visual one. Music only exists in real time passing into and out of existence on the air which it disturbs so that our ears can perceive it. To learn it requires memorization, repetition, and lots of practice. This is immediate memory.

Then there is nostalgia. This word was coined by a Swiss doctor in 1688 to describe a malady common among Swiss mercenaries fighting in France and Italy. It had been called the "mal du Suisse" or Swiss sickness, but Dr. Johannes Hofer more precisely described it with two Greek words, "nostos" and "algos," that when combined meant "homesickness." This was triggered by the singing of songs that revived the memory of the Alpine valleys from which the mercenaries had been recruited. Rousseau, in his *Dictionary of Music*, wrote that this became such a serious problem, leading to desertion, illness, or death, that the mercenaries were forbidden to sing these songs altogether.[2]

---

2   Jean-Jacques Rousseau, *Dictionary of Music*, trans. William Waring (London: J. Murray, 1779), 266–67.

What I am calling historical memory is distinguished from both the mnemonic and nostalgia by its recollection of actual events in which people took part. While a mnemonic may aid in performing a task and nostalgia may be a longing for a mythical place, the marking of great struggles such as uprisings, revolutions, or civil wars is a specific function of memory that, like the rest, is served by music. The classic example is the national anthem but it is not confined to this. Indeed, a fundamental purpose of balladry the world over is to remember the battles, victories, and defeats of oppressed social classes and ethnic groups. Precisely when History is being written by the victor, it is to song we have to look for the perspective and experience of the defeated. Or, to put it another way, songs remind us how temporary victory and defeat actually are. Thus, songs evoke a spirit of resistance, reviving and renewing it, undaunted and unafraid.

This is of considerable importance to musicians learning their craft. All the skills that must be gained in order to perform well and that take years to acquire are specific in both mechanical and cultural ways. Learning to play the guitar, for example, requires that one learn not only the chords, scales, tunings, and rhythms particular to the instrument but also those that are particular to certain forms such as blues, jazz, Irish or flamenco, and so forth. This necessarily includes learning songs and other compositions that comprise the canon or archive that make up a musical idiom. Now all of this might go without saying except for the fact that what is often required of musicians is merely formal accuracy or good technique. In fact, we often ignore the feelings and ideas the song was originally intended to convey. Thus, expanding repertoire or increasing virtuosity takes the place of feeling. What this process forgets is that music's most important quality is spiritual in that it evokes powerful emotions, it moves us. It is, therefore, of utmost importance that musicians not only learn the mechanical and formal aspects of performance but that they learn what inspired the creation of the songs or compositions they are to play in the first place. Blues is not just a style. It is a library of responses, emotional and intellectual, to the conditions faced by generations of African Americans. More particularly, it conveys, often in coded language, a wisdom gained through hard experience under slavery and ever since.

The same can be said of many other forms, for example, Irish music. When James Connolly published his *Songs of Freedom* in 1907, he prefaced the collection with this statement: "No revolutionary movement is complete without its poetical expression. If such a movement has caught hold of the imagination of the masses, they will seek a vent in song for the aspirations, the fears and hopes, the loves and hatreds engendered by the struggle."[3] Now, Connolly's statement is itself a part of history, but its relevance here is that it accurately expresses one crucial component in the development of Irish music and in a particular way: during an eight-hundred-year struggle against English conquest there were many who consciously sought to use music in the service of this struggle, thereby enriching music in the process. One song typifying an entire legacy is "The Rising of the Moon." This song was written long after the events it depicts, namely the uprising of 1798, in order to inspire another attempt, the Fenian rebellion of 1867.

> How well they fought for poor old Ireland
> And full bitter, was their fate
> Oh what glorious pride and sorrow
> Fills the name of ninety-eight.
>
> Yet thank god while hearts are beating
> Each man bears a burning wound
> We will follow in their footsteps
> At the rising of the moon.

Now how can one hope to capture the feelings that went into this song's composition and perform them today without knowing at least something of the history involved?

It might be argued, of course, that this is the job of the ethnomusicologist, the folklorist, or even a producer like T-Bone Burnett selecting songs for a movie such as *O Brother Where Art Thou?*. It might further be argued that musicians should simply play well and express their own feelings through whatever compositional form they choose. What is most authentic and convincing in any case is one's own passion and skill, not how well or poorly informed one is about history or politics. These are valid arguments with which I generally agree. But they cannot be isolated from the real situation in which musicians find themselves at any particular time, including right now. Not only is a great deal of rich experience written out of the historical record but many formal attributes of the music of oppressed people are appropriated to be used against them. This is nowhere more clearly demonstrated than in the history of the United States, both in political terms and in terms of how music was turned into a commodity by the music industry. The question was eloquently addressed by Duke

---

3   http://www.marxists.org/archive/connolly/index.htm.

Ellington, who, when asked to comment on Gershwin's *Porgy and Bess* said, "Grand music and a swell play, I guess, but the two don't go together . . . the music did not hitch with the mood and spirit of the story," adding that "it does not use the Negro musical idiom" (from a 1935 interview in *New Theatre* magazine). Ellington did far more than comment, however. He devoted his own creative effort to *Jump for Joy*, a highly successful musical of 1941. In *Jump for Joy*, Ellington directly addressed the representations of black Americans in musical theater:

> Now, every Broadway colored show,
> According to tradition,
> Must be a carbon copy
> Of the previous edition.
> With the truth discreetly muted,
> And the accent on the brasses,
> The punch that should be present
> In a colored show, alas, is
> Disinfected with magnolia
> And dripping with molasses.
> In other words,
> We're shown to you
> Through Stephen Foster's glasses.[4]

This is one small but formidable example of the general problem. Musicians are placed in a peculiar position of being the bearers of historical memory at the same time it is often their fate to seek employment by those who'd most like to erase that memory. While the schoolbooks and mass media may succeed in carrying out this erasure, it is virtually impossible to do so with music. In fact, a crucial component of what produced the musical renaissance of the 1960s was the realization on the part of a young generation of white people that the main source of their beloved music was the African American and more specifically, the suffering, struggling, and rejoicing of this people. Clearly, the political struggle for civil rights and later for black liberation was the main reason people were made aware of this fact and the howling hypocrisies it exposed. Still, music played such an indispensable role in the lives and aspirations

---

4   Interview in *New Theatre* and song lyrics quoted in Michael Denning, *The Cultural Front* (New York: Verso, 1997), 309–19.

of black Americans that there was no way even the most apolitical musician could remain unaware of the connection between music and history, particularly the history that was being made at that very moment. Besides, the barriers of segregation were becoming less and less effective due in large part to music, particularly its transmission by radio. Radio allowed young people to compare for themselves Pat Boone's versions of songs written and performed by Little Richard. Race records, only recently renamed Rhythm and Blues, became the prized possessions of hipsters and aficionados, and soon thereafter the crucial element in any dance party. This had, moreover, a significant effect on impressionable young minds. As Steve Van Zandt recently pointed out, "Little Richard opened his mouth and out came liberation."[5] Here was a sound and excitement that could not be contained by legislation, censorship or banning and burning records. Although such suppression was indeed attempted—and is an important subject in its own right—the point here is that musicians found themselves in a vortex of social conflict that affected music as such. In other words, one could not play any of the burgeoning varieties of rock music without coming into contact with these controversies and in one way or another taking a position. This produced some timeless music that was, at the time of its creation, quite innovative. Outstanding examples include Sly and the Family Stone, Santana, and Tower of Power—all of whom broke new musical ground by deliberately challenging prevailing norms of what a band should look like, what styles of music could be combined, and how the turmoil in society should be addressed. From Sly's "Stand" to Tower's "What Is Hip?" it was demonstrated how one could simultaneously honor musical traditions while doing something genuinely new.

Of course this had precedents in previous generations, and it was certainly not the case that the generation coming of age in the 1960s somehow fell from the sky. In fact, it was to a large extent the influence of the folk music revival, which reached its apex in the first half of the 1960s, that produced two crucial effects on what transpired in the last half of that decade and beyond. First, there was the enduring connection between music and the labor movement, which would continue with the subsequent peace and civil rights movements. From Joe Hill in the early twentieth century through Woody Guthrie, Pete Seeger, and many others, a long, unbroken tradition had firmly established a connection between music and popular struggle. This was, moreover, based on the music miners, textile workers, sharecroppers, and

---

5   Steve Van Zandt's induction speech for the Hollies at the Rock & Roll Hall of Fame, March 15, 2010, New York City.

other laborers were making themselves. The second point is that even when some practitioners of this music became commercially successful, the tension between the slick, sanitized mainstream version and the raw eloquence of the original produced a similar effect among young musicians as had the comparison of white covers of black songs. An entire generation became increasingly sensitive to the abyss that separates the genuine from the fake, the authentic from the phony. Even largely innocuous and ingenuous acts such as the Kingston Trio or We Five were viewed with derision when compared to the New Lost City Ramblers, Bob Dylan, Joan Baez, Odetta, or Buffy Sainte-Marie. The dividing line had been drawn with such creative force that even when Rock 'n' Roll overwhelmed the folk music revival, rejecting many of its musical constraints, the question of the authentic vs. the fake remained a fundamental criterion of music and society as a whole. If proof is needed there's none better than Dylan's unforgettable denunciation:

> Money doesn't talk, it swears,
> Obscenity, who really cares,
> Propaganda, all is phony[6]

Now forty years later this has a bearing on the question of music and historical memory for the obvious reason that this period is now history which music carries forward even as it is being forgotten or deliberately obscured in much public discourse. After all, music making was altered in significant ways during that period which for better or for worse has had enduring impact on music itself. The point here, however, is that there are specific historical lessons taught by music that both affected popular consciousness on a large scale then and can still be learned from today. Noteworthy examples can be drawn from a vast number of songs such as Dylan's "George Jackson" or John Coltrane's "Afro Blue," from Nina Simone's "Mississippi Goddam" to the Mothers' "Trouble Comin' Everyday," not to mention a host of social commentary for which Zappa was then and is now deservedly admired. Perhaps nothing better represents this than the opening and closing performances in the movie of the Woodstock festival, namely Richie Havens singing "Handsome Johnny"—a pointedly historical text—and Jimi Hendrix's stunning version of the "Star Spangled Banner"—a wordless statement, powerfully evoking everything entangled in that moment of war and revolution. And these are only the world-renowned markers

---

6   Bob Dylan, "It's Alright, Ma (I'm Only Bleeding)."

by which a much larger field is indicated. It should not be forgotten that in the main, anonymous multitudes form the rich soil of music making and of history, the driving force ultimately responsible for whatever remains for us to savor, enjoy and learn from. This is not simply an obligatory nod to the democratic masses, either. If the historical memory that music shelters and passes on contains anything at all it is the memory of great popular movements for liberation. Through such music we are reminded of heroes who were people like us, courage that we too may summon and futures that are better than the present or the mythical past.

Cognizant of this fact, one of the main aims of the music industry, from its inception, was to replace this particular function of music with something else. Instead of historical memory, we are offered novelty and nostalgia. This goes back to the origins of Tin Pan Alley and its predecessors in minstrel shows and vaudeville. It is demonstrated again by the industry's treatment of ragtime and the coon song. That this was systematic and deliberate is beyond any doubt.[7] That musicians in particular have suffered the consequences is worthy of another discussion in its own right. But suffice it to say that norms established by weekly hit parades, massive promotional budgets, and lavish expenditure to manufacture celebrity have created a situation in which the feverish recycling of clichés takes the place of genuine innovation and the pathetic longings for a nonexistent homeland take the place of people's aspirations for a better life. These are the twin incubi on the shoulder of every musician working at his or her craft and have to be confronted head on. The least one can do is to disabuse themselves of the notion that quality or ability have anything at all to do with how one is judged by the music industry. Indeed, taking hold of what music tells of history can be a useful shield against the unalloyed nonsense loudly proclaimed by cretins and bean counters as if they were the wise representatives of the "people." As if they give a damn about anything except profitability.

Instead, all of us who love music should meet the challenge posed to Hesiod by the Muses. We should aspire to more than being mere "bellies" or animal appetites. We should call upon the Muses to tell the truth and not convincing lies. We should learn from the great reservoir of music that celebrates the real heroism human beings are capable of. And, even as we compose new music and attempt to break new ground, let's draw inspiration from the feelings and ideas that arise from lived experience. Our own as well as those who've gone before.

---

7   See David Suisman, *Selling Sounds* (Cambridge, MA: Harvard University Press, 2009).

ACKNOWLEDGMENTS

We especially want to thank the following people for their invaluable assistance:

Jay Blakesberg for assistance in gaining access to Jim Marshall's lovely photo of Sarah Ogan Gunning and Pete Seeger

Tiny Seeger for providing photos of Sarah Ogan Gunning, Jim Garland, and John Handcox from her father's personal collection

Eli Smith for his help in conceiving this project and launching it at the Brooklyn Folk Festival

Steve Garabedian and Franz Morrissey for their insightful reading and thoughtful criticism in the preparation of this book

ABOUT THE EDITORS

MAT CALLAHAN AND YVONNE MOORE HAVE BEEN PARTNERS IN LIFE AND WORK FOR TWENTY years. Their collaboration began in 1998 working on Yvonne's album *Between You and I*. Since then they have performed and recorded together in various formations, including those listed below. While each continues to pursue their individual projects, they regularly perform together as a duet. Tours have taken them to the United States, Ireland, England, France, Germany, and Italy.

Please visit the following websites for more information:
http://matcallahan.com/
http://www.yvonne-moore.ch/

Discography
Songs of Freedom—the James Connolly Songs of Freedom Band
Welcome—Mat &Yvonne
Burn the Boogeyman—Mat & Yvonne

Albums by Mat Callahan
A Wild Bouquet
San Francisco
Testimony

Albums by Yvonne Moore
Walkin' the Blues
Between You and I
Nomad
Put Out the Trash
Blue Wisdom, Vols. 1 & 2

ABOUT PM

PM Press was founded at the end of 2007 by a small collection of folks with decades of publishing, media, and organizing experience. PM Press co-conspirators have published and distributed hundreds of books, pamphlets, CDs, and DVDs. Members of PM have founded enduring book fairs, spearheaded victorious tenant organizing campaigns, and worked closely with bookstores, academic conferences, and even rock bands to deliver political and challenging ideas to all walks of life. We're old enough to know what we're doing and young enough to know what's at stake.

We create radical and stimulating fiction and non-fiction books, pamphlets, T-shirts, visual and audio materials to educate, entertain, and inspire you. We aim to distribute these through every available channel with every available technology—whether that means you are seeing anarchist classics at our bookfair stalls; reading our latest vegan cookbook at the café; downloading geeky fiction e-books; or digging new music and timely videos from our website.

PM Press is always on the lookout for talented and skilled volunteers, artists, activists, and writers to work with. If you have a great idea for a project or can contribute in some way, please get in touch.

PM Press
PO Box 23912
Oakland CA 94623
510-658-3906
www.pmpress.org

PM Press in Europe
europe@pmpress.org
www.pmpress.org.uk

FRIENDS OF PM

These are indisputably momentous times—the financial system is melting down globally and the Empire is stumbling. Now more than ever there is a vital need for radical ideas.

In the many years since its founding—and on a mere shoestring—PM Press has risen to the formidable challenge of publishing and distributing knowledge and entertainment for the struggles ahead. With hundreds of releases to date, we have published an impressive and stimulating array of literature, art, music, politics, and culture. Using every available medium, we've succeeded in connecting those hungry for ideas and information to those putting them into practice.

Friends of PM allows you to directly help impact, amplify, and revitalize the discourse and actions of radical writers, filmmakers, and artists. It provides us with a stable foundation from which we can build upon our early successes and provides a much-needed subsidy for the materials that can't necessarily pay their own way. You can help make that happen—and receive every new title automatically delivered to your door once a month—by joining as a Friend of PM Press. And, we'll throw in a free T-shirt when you sign up.

Here are your options:

- $30 a month: Get all books and pamphlets plus 50% discount on all webstore purchases
- $40 a month: Get all PM Press releases (including CDs and DVDs) plus 50% discount on all webstore purchases
- $100 a month: Superstar—Everything plus PM merchandise, free downloads, and 50% discount on all webstore purchases

For those who can't afford $30 or more a month, we have SUSTAINER RATES at $15, $10, and $5. Sustainers get a free PM Press T-shirt and a 50% discount on all purchases from our website.

Your Visa or Mastercard will be billed once a month, until you tell us to stop. Or until our efforts succeed in bringing the revolution around. Or the financial meltdown of Capital makes plastic redundant. Whichever comes first.

SONGS OF FREEDOM
The James Connolly
Songbook
Edited by Mat Callahan Preface
by Theo Dorgan Foreword by
James Connolly Heron
$12.95 • 6x9 • 96 pages
ISBN: 978-1-60486-826-5

Songs of Freedom is the songbook edited by James Connolly from 1907. Connolly's introduction is better known than the collection, containing his oft-quoted maxim: "Until the movement is marked by the joyous, defiant singing of revolutionary songs, it lacks one of the most distinctive marks of a popular revolutionary movement, it is the dogma of a few and not the faith of the multitude." Though most of the songs were of Irish derivation, the songbook itself was published in New York and directed to the American working class, explicitly internationalist in its aims.

Songs of Freedom is a celebration of the life and work of James Connolly, the Irish revolutionary socialist martyred by the British government for his role in the Easter Rising of 1916. It is at once a collection of stirring revolutionary songs and a vital historical document. For the first time in a hundred years, readers will find the original *Songs of Freedom* as well as the *1919 Connolly Souvenir* program published for a concert commemorating Connolly's birth. Both are reproduced exactly as they originally appeared, providing a fascinating glimpse of the workers' struggle at the beginning of the last century. To complete the picture is included the *James Connolly Songbook of 1972*, which contains not only the most complete selection of Connolly's lyrics, but also historical background essential to understanding the context in which the songs were written and performed.

THE EXPLOSION OF DEFERRED DREAMS
Musical Renaissance and
Social Revolution in San
Francisco, 1965–1975
Mat Callahan
$22.95 • 6x9 • 352 pages
ISBN: 978-1-62963-231-5

The Explosion of Deferred Dreams offers a critical re-examination of the interwoven political and musical happenings in San Francisco in the Sixties. Author, musician, and native San Franciscan Mat Callahan explores the dynamic links between the Black Panthers and Sly and the Family Stone, the United Farm Workers and Santana, the Indian Occupation of Alcatraz and the San Francisco Mime Troupe, and the New Left and the counterculture.

Callahan's meticulous, impassioned arguments both expose and reframe the political and social context for the San Francisco Sound and the vibrant subcultural uprisings with which it is associated. Using dozens of original interviews, primary sources, and personal experiences, the author shows how the intense interplay of artistic and political movements put San Francisco, briefly, in the forefront of a worldwide revolutionary upsurge.

A must-read for any musician, historian, or person who "was there" (or longed to have been), *The Explosion of Deferred Dreams* is substantive and provocative, inviting us to reinvigorate our historical sense-making of an era that assumes a mythic role in the contemporary American zeitgeist.

SONGS OF FREEDOM CD
The James Connolly Songs of
Freedom Band
$14.95
ISBN: 978-1-60486-831-9

From the rollicking welcome of "A Festive Song" to the defiant battle cry of "Watchword of Labor," *Songs of Freedom* accomplishes the difficult task of making contemporary music out of old revolutionary songs. Far from the archival preservation of embalmed corpses, the inspired performance of a rocking band turns the timeless lyrics of James Connolly into timely manifestos for today's young rebels. As Connolly himself repeatedly urged, nothing can replace the power of music to raise the fighting spirit of the oppressed.

Giving expression to Connolly's internationalism, musical influences ranging from traditional Irish airs to American rhythm and blues are combined here in refreshing creativity. As for the songs themselves, nine have lyrics by Connolly, three were written about Connolly, and one, "The Red Flag," was chosen by Connolly to be in the original *Songs of Freedom* songbook of 1907, subsequently becoming a classic song of Labor. The instrumentation is acoustic: guitars, uilleann pipes, whistles, fiddle, accordion, and Irish harp, as well as drums and bass.

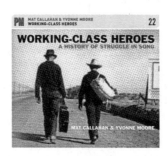

WORKING-CLASS HEROES CD
Mat Callahan and Yvonne
Moore
$14.95
ISBN: 978-1-62963-762-4

The most essential music is conceived by real human beings: ordinary, anonymous, often poor—people who stood up and joined together to fight injustice and institutional oppression. This is the story of *Working-Class Heroes*, a collection of American working-class, pre–World War II folk songs revived by Mat Callahan & Yvonne Moore. Here the duo presents 20 songs written by both by folk canon heavyweights and lesser-known but equally gifted songwriters . Both beautiful and emotionally arresting, the album is a collection of stories as much as songs—stories of the women and men who (sometimes literally) gave their lives to emancipate the working class.